WEAVING DREAMS

WEAVING DREAMS

Ima's Memoir of Empowerment

A Life Entwined with Manipur's Rich Legacy

SONIA OINAM

KONARK

Konark Publishers Pvt. Ltd
206, First Floor,
Peacock Lane, Shahpur Jat,
New Delhi 110 049
+91-11-4105 5065
india@konarkpublishers.com, us@konarkpublishers.com
www.konarkpublishers.com

The photographs used in this book are from the personal collections of the author.

ISBN: 978-81-973432-4-7
Edited by Dipali Singh
Jacket design by Sanjeev Kumar
Cover Image © Sonia Oinam
Typeset by K.K. Gusain
Printed and bound at Saurbh Printers Pvt. Ltd, Greater Noida

This book is a tribute

to

my late mother,

Oinam Ongbi Memcha

Contents

Foreword by Jarnail Singh, IAS (Retd) ix

Message by Binalakshmi Nepram xi

Prologue xiii

1. Beginnings 1
2. A Resolution 10
3. Sleep a Bit, Eat a Bit (*Tumba Machet, Chaba Machet*) 17
4. The Initial Struggle 31
5. Our Family and Lessons Learnt 43
6. Demise of *Baba* 62
7. *Ima* and *Ima Keithel* 71
8. The Lone Journey 91
9. Lighter Moments 107
10. A Friend, Philosopher, and Guide 125
11. Farewell 139

Epilogue 144

Glossary 149

References 155

Index 157

About the Author 166

Foreword

This tribute by Sonia Oinam recounts the heroic tale of her *Ima* (mother), Oinam *Ongbi* Memcha, who was born in a poor family in Manipur. From a young age, she learnt that success could only be achieved through diligence, perseverance, discipline, and dedication. As she grew up, she developed a passion for weaving and integrated her life with the famous *Ima Keithel* (Mothers' Market) of Imphal. Through her entrepreneurial initiatives and micro marketing strategies, she not only supported fellow weavers but also significantly contributed to her family's income.

The narrative vividly portrays the remarkable qualities and unbending spirit of Oinam *Ongbi* Memcha. Even though she faced financial stress quite often and lost her husband in a tragic accident, she was able to bring up a well-knit family due to her 'never say die' attitude. She stayed focused on her family, co-workers at the *Ima* Market, and relatives, showing an intense involvement in her work and complete commitment to her family. The way she imparted knowledge and instilled ethical values in her children—through stories and earthly wisdom drawn from real-life examples—ensured that they became valuable assets to society. The book contains touching moments that underscore the inner strength of *Ima*'s character and her fortitude.

After reading the book, one realises the importance of the *Ima* Market to Manipuri society, particularly the women weavers, in generating employment as well as supplementing family incomes since time immemorial in Manipur. During my service in Manipur from 1975 to 2008 and subsequent assignments there until 2020, I witnessed firsthand how the *Ima* Market remained a major centre of economic activities for women weavers in the state.

An integral part of *Ima* Oinam *Ongbi* Memcha's life revolved around weaving and then selling exquisite woollen shawls and other garments in the *Ima* Market, reflecting the industriousness of Manipuri women weavers and vendors.

This book by Sonia Oinam is a must-read for all those interested in understanding the difficulties, struggles, and pivotal roles of *Ima*s in meaningfully enriching their families in Manipur. It portrays them not only as devoted mothers but also as financial providers.

New Delhi

Jarnail Singh, IAS (Retd.)
Former Chief Secretary of Manipur

Message

I was very moved as I went through this beautifully written memoir—a testimony of a daughter's love for her beloved mother who struggled against odds with grace and dignity to raise her family and see her children truly bloom. While it is a deeply personal family narrative, it is also the story of the extraordinary *Imas*—the resilient women and mothers of Manipur with their defining presence manifested in their weavings, herbal expertise, pottery, craftsmanship, indigenous cuisine and products in the legendary Ima Keithel, or Mother's Market, for over 500 years. They have continued to be the central soul and heartbeat of our state and civilization for over 2,000 years.

This memoir is a work of great love and deep faith, an extraordinary affirmation of the amazing grit, spirit, strength, and resilience of not only Ima Memcha but of all the mothers of Manipur. They are our hope, our past, our present, and, most of all, our future that holds the key to building a strong, resilient, and diverse Manipur.

Binalakshmi Nepram
Founder-Director, Manipur Women Gun Survivors Network/CAFI

Prologue

The love that a mother nurtures in her heart for her child is unique. From the time she is carrying her child in her womb until the moment she gives birth, she bears all physical hardships with a smile. When a child is born, family members are overjoyed, but they often ignore the physical weakness, fatigue, and mental anguish that a mother goes through after giving birth. It is crucial to understand that she requires both physical and emotional support as she cares for her entirely dependent baby. Despite the challenges, a mother must exhibit strength, tending to the baby's needs day and nights, and remaining alert to every cry. Like a devoted shadow, a mother keeps a constant vigil over her child, attending to each breath and step. In a mother's heart, her child always remains her little one, forever seeking the comfort and love only a mother can give. This truth holds for my *Ima* (meaning mother in Manipuri) and for every other mother out there.

Ima was a determined and hard-working person—her biggest strength was her strong belief in herself. Her commitment to duty and hard work guided her through life's struggles. Beginning as a weaver in her youth, she later forayed into *Ima Keithel*, Manipur's renowned market run only by women, and established herself as a woollen shawl vendor. She tirelessly collaborated with weavers to produce the traditional shawls of Manipur, empowering herself financially and uplifting all those who were part of her weaving network.

This memoir is an attempt to share the remarkable story of *Ima*, who always showed immense courage throughout her life. Her story of resilience in the face of adversity will inspire all those striving each day for livelihood to courageously tackle life's challenges. Recognising the struggle many individuals—regardless of age or gender—face in maintaining clarity of purpose and preserving their self-esteem, I believe this book will motivate readers to believe in themselves, enhance their self-worth, and champion self-reliance in others.

Born into a poor family, *Ima* was raised by parents who had to struggle hard to support the family. She learnt from them how to face life's challenges with courage and determination, and how to make her own decisions while upholding her self-esteem and inner strength. *Ima* approached the difficulties with a smile. Her strong faith in herself and her ability to work hard helped her to triumph over hardship and negativity.

She taught us, her children, the virtues of living a fulfilling life, which meant discipline, dedication to duty, and perseverance. Above all, she taught us to have a strong belief and faith in the Divine, as well as to remain focused on our objectives.

I vividly remember a conversation with *Ima* after reading the *Bhagavad Gita*. "Why are we born? Is it to pray and devote ourselves to God?" I inquired. She replied, "I believe that true faith in God should be felt—a belief that He is always with us, aiding us in fulfilling our daily duties. It's a faith that teaches us to love our neighbours, to have positive thoughts and to do good to all, regardless how they treat us. For me, work is worship. God wants us to do our duties, which will show our deep devotion to Him." And true to her words, she believed no matter what circumstances she might be in, God always helped her out. She made me realise the true meaning of worshipping God. I owe all my achievements to her, my beloved *Ima.*

What truly differentiated *Ima* from others were her indomitable spirit and her willpower to change her life and achieve her aims. She did not fear failure or hard work. What she feared was drowning with weak, helpless people who gave up easily, bemoaning their fate and circumstances. Though she faced many hardships while raising us, she never gave up her responsibilities. Even when people doubted our ability to face the future after our father's death, *Ima* believed in her vision for us. Because of her dedication, persistence, and hard work, we were able to cross every obstacle that came our way.

Ima created her own identity as a successful handloom weaver and entrepreneur. Through imparting her traditional knowledge and skills, *Ima* gave an opportunity to others to pick up this craft and make a living. The weavers who worked with her later established their own businesses, carving out their own paths. She courageously took risks to advance and grow, turning her shortcomings into strengths. The promotion of women's economic empowerment through a supportive network of weavers is fundamental to the weaving community. I still clearly recall *Ima*'s close relationship with her fellow weavers despite diligently working on her loom. They shared a common struggle and triumphed over numerous obstacles together. As I document *Ima*'s story, I am also excited to shed light on the weaving community in Manipur. To a Manipuri woman, mastering the art of handloom weaving entails more than simply earning a living; it embodies her identity and dignity, and speaks of her self-reliance. This memoir further highlights the remarkable dynamics of *Ima Keithel*, the largest market in Asia that is run entirely by women and is located in Imphal, the capital of Manipur state. It explores the deep connection *Ima* and many other Manipuri women have with this market.

One of *Ima*'s deepest regrets was her inability to read and write because of the poverty that forced her to drop out of school at an early age. She often lamented, "If only I could read and write, my life would have been different." Recognising the transformative power of education for both men and women, *Ima* viewed its absence as a significant barrier to her personal growth. Therefore, her primary goal became ensuring her children received an education.

As she shared her life experiences with us, she frequently expressed a profound desire to pen down her own story. Now, fulfilling her wish has become my solemn pledge—one that I am committed to honouring.

Since 2012, I have been documenting *Ima*'s stories. Our post-dinner conversations often revolved around her tales of struggle and perseverance. With her demise, *Ima*'s firsthand account of her life's journey remained unfinished. Yet, in every chapter, I have strived to capture the essence of her storytelling. My goal has been to recall her words and convey her narrative through the vivid memories etched in my mind and heart.

While I understand that many chapters of her life will forever remain incomplete and untold, I felt compelled to recount *Ima*'s journey as authentically as she shared it with me. I must acknowledge that my efforts would have been incomplete without the invaluable help and feedback from my siblings—Kemila, Robert, Promila, Dhanabati, and Tiken—for which I am deeply grateful.

Throughout this memoir, I have used some Manipuri words. Their meanings are provided in the Glossary at the end of the book, in the hope that they enrich and deepen the understanding of readers.

As readers go through the various chapters of this memoir, they will witness the trials and triumphs that shaped *Ima*'s life. Always guided by her inner voice and clarity of mind, she navigated from early setbacks to self-reliance, demonstrating a resilient entrepreneurial spirit. She grappled with the challenges of motherhood and widowhood with remarkable courage, overcoming every obstacle in her path. I am confident her story will inspire readers to believe in themselves and move forward with fortitude and determination.

I am deeply grateful to my husband, Yaiphaba Longjam, and my sister-in-law, Inoulembi Longjam, for their patient proofreading, as well as my in-laws for their constant support. I also extend my heartfelt thanks to my sister, Dr Promila Oinam, and my friend, Anuradha Usham, for their meticulous proofreading and insightful suggestions, which have truly enriched the essence of this book.

I am thankful to Dr Sanghamitra Dhar for our reading sessions and invaluable feedback on the manuscript.

I also express gratitude to Shri Jarnail Singh IAS (retired), former Chief Secretary of Manipur, for generously sharing his expertise and experiences in enhancing *Ima Keithel* during his tenure in Manipur (as detailed in Chapter 7) and for his support towards the publication of this memoir.

Lastly, I am thankful to Konark Publishers for their guidance and support in making the publication of this memoir possible.

Imphal **Sonia Oinam**

1

Beginnings

My mother was affectionately known as "Memcha" among her family and friends, although her birth name was Satyavama. To us, she was lovingly referred to as *Ima,* which translates to "mother" in Meiteilon, the language of Manipur. She was born on 29 June 1947 to Kshetrimayum Tolumu and Kshetrimayum Ongbi Tonshiza, who lived in a locality called Kshetri Leikai, in Singjamei Chingamakha, Imphal. Imphal, nestled in the heart of Manipur—a hilly state of Northeast India—is a valley secured and surrounded by lush green hill ranges. It was in this picturesque land that *Ima* was born, amidst a community known for its hard work and courage displayed by its women.

Later in life, she reaped the fruits of her perseverance by owning a *potpham* (stall) in the *Ima Keithel,* renowned as the *Ima* Market—the world-famous and all-women market in Imphal. Here, she specialised in selling traditional Manipuri shawls and stoles. These woollen shawls are exquisite handloom products woven by talented weavers of Manipur and feature unique designs and motifs.

Ima always kept an extra collection of her woollen shawls at our home, carefully packed in separate bags according to their categories, colours, and designs. She diligently stocked up the shawls throughout the year, ensuring she was well-prepared for the winter sales season.

After dinner, *Ima* used to relax by sitting on a *kouna* mat in our living room, watching television. I would switch channels for her, knowing she enjoyed either Manipuri or Bollywood movies. If none piqued her interest, she preferred to stitch her handloom shawls. These shawls, woven by skilled artisans on handlooms, generally come in two halves that needed stitching together. She would select a *leiroom,* a traditional Manipuri shawl, from her collections and, as she worked, regale us with stories of her life. She would feel overwhelmed with emotions whenever she recounted her struggles and triumphs.

It was during these moments that I would hastily jot down everything she shared about her experiences.

Ima recounted how her mother would travel to Kakching, about 40 km from Imphal, to purchase locally grown vegetables. "She would buy these vegetables in Kakching and then sell them at Imphal's Singjamei *Keithel* and *Ima Keithel.* We affectionately called our father *Baazi.* He was a construction worker, tall and well-built. He was a member of the *Nupa Pala,* a troupe of male performers engaged in *Nat Sankirtan*—a traditional form of ritual drumming, dancing, and singing performed at weddings and during *shraddha* rites. *Baazi* was deeply religious and also a very strict father. We were all afraid of him, but adored and revered him immensely."

Ima was the youngest among six siblings. She had two elder brothers, Joykumar and Ramkumar, as well as three elder sisters—

Ekashini, Bino, and Sakhi. *Ima* continued, "Ekashini was the eldest, while Bino was second to her, followed by Sakhi who was more like a friend to me. She was fair and beautiful, a light-hearted person who enjoyed life to the fullest. We would weave together, but sometimes she would skip this and go out to watch movies. When she came home late, I would cover up for her so that she did not get a scolding from our *Baazi*. She was very caring, helpful, and loving.

"My eldest brother Joykumar was the tallest among all of us and was a calm and kind-hearted person. Ramkumar was a very obedient son and feared our *Baazi* a lot. He never dared to speak loudly to him, but would stand behind the wall and whisper what he wanted to say. *Baazi* would listen patiently to him and always gave him what he wanted. I remember how he would carry me on his back and showed me around Singjamei while we waited for our mother's return from the Singjamei *Keithel*. My brothers pampered me and loved me dearly. We all lived in one big house, a *yumjao*, a traditional house with its architectural style distinctly that of the Meiteis."

Ima reminisced about an incident when her father imparted a lesson that she never forgot. "My sister Sakhi and I were quarrelling over husking rice. We were both consumed by anger and sulked so much that our mother had to step in and cook the rice herself that day. Our careless quarrel had left rice husks unremoved during winnowing, and due to our mother's weak eyesight, she also didn't notice them. When the cooking was over, brown husks surfaced in the rice and became visible. Exhausted from his day, *Baazi*'s patience snapped when he sat down to eat and found the husks. He took out a handful of them from the cooked rice and instructed us to eat it with the husks intact. The taste of those husks taught us a valuable lesson—we had to do our daily chores with mindfulness. From that day onwards, we did our chores meticulously, not letting any trivial emotions get in our way.

"We were a poor family. My parents struggled and worked hard for a livelihood and to meet our basic needs. My mother sold vegetables, while *Baazi* would either go for construction work or for *Sankirtan* engagements. Whatever they earned for the day would suffice primarily for *chengjen wanba*,[1] which is purchasing rice, our staple diet. However, our income was insufficient to cover family expenses, education, clothing, and other miscellaneous needs. So, I had no choice but to drop out of school at a young age."

After *Ima* had to stop attending school due to financial constraints, she turned her focus to handlooms and embroidery. "We were struggling financially, and even affording decent clothing was difficult," she recalled. "My mother owned and regularly used a *kon*, our Manipuri loom, where my sister Sakhi and I learnt weaving from her. We also practiced embroidery and knitting embroidery and knitting in our *pheesashang*, our work space. We used a fine thread called *karan lang*, which we prepared by boiling, stretching, drying, and spinning on a *tareng*, a wooden spinning wheel, to weave sarees and other clothes."

Despite their hard work, the income from their efforts was modest and mostly went towards groceries, *chengjen wanba*, and other necessities. "I never wanted to burden my family, so I worked hard to contribute financially," *Ima* explained. "Through this, I found fulfilment and began to develop self-respect. Early on, I learnt the importance of safeguarding my own self-esteem."

"As my earnings gradually increased, I was able to buy and wear my favourite clothes and pursue activities I couldn't before," *Ima* reminisced.

---

1 Rice is the staple food of the people of Manipur. *Chengjen wanba* is a term used for purchasing rice and signifies the daily struggle for survival among common people in Manipuri society, particularly for daily wage earners.

Ima's eldest brother, Joykumar, found success in business in Kohima, Nagaland, and later joined a paper press in Imphal, where he worked until retirement. Ramkumar found employment at the All India Radio office at Imphal. "After my brothers married and began living separately, our family started to drift apart," *Ima* reflected. "After Ekashini and Sakhi got married, I decided to move in with Joykumar's family, while my parents stayed with Ramkumar.

"I used to listen to the recitations of the *Bhagavad Gita* at our Brahmin neighbour's house. My family practiced both Sanamahism, the indigenous religion of the Meiteis, and Vaishnavism, which involves the worship of Lord Krishna and Radha. Being born into a *Kshetrimayum* (*Kshatriya*) family, we were inclined to Vaishnavism. Whenever my sister-in-law's brother travelled outside Manipur for business, I would often ask him to bring idols of Lord Ganesha and Goddess Lakshmi for me. I worshipped these deities with deep faith, believing they brought prosperity and good fortune into my life."

One evening, while we sat together talking after dinner, *Ima* fell silent for a moment. Then, she shared a touching story about her eldest sister Ekashini, a memory still vivid in her mind. We affectionately referred Aunt Ekashini, much older than *Ima,* as *Imabok Kabok Yonbi,* the aunt who sold puffed rice. In her kitchen, *Imabok* always kept two large tin cans filled with puffed rice for sale. Whenever we visited her, we would eagerly rush to those cans, grabbing handfuls of puffed rice and relishing every morsel to our heart's content.

Ima recounted the story, saying, "*Madi rashi na yommi*, her beauty was captivating. As a young girl, I used to hover around Ekashini during her romantic dates. She was deeply in love with a young man, but our parents arranged her marriage to a man from Samurou, about 15 km from Imphal. Sadly, her husband passed away, and she returned home. Taking his chance, the young man, a humble and kind person, persistently urged her to elope with him. Despite my sister's shy and soft-spoken nature, she was also firm. I remember her bidding farewell to her love, quietly explaining that she was a widow while he was still unmarried. She stood her ground, guided by her principles and values, and told him to forget her. He respected her decision but waited for a long time, hoping she might change her mind.

"However, fate took a cruel turn one day when another man abducted Ekashini against her will. In those days, incidents of *nupiphaba* (abduction of women or eloping with them without their consent) were common. Women usually would marry their abductor after elopement, but in this case, it was a true kidnapping without her consent—forcing her into marriage with the abductor. This unfortunate twist of fate tore her away from the one who cherished her. These tragic events deeply affected me emotionally and made me cautious in matters of love.

"In my youth, I learnt that love wasn't always straightforward. I came to understand that trust was more important than love itself. There was a time when I was infatuated with a boy, caught up in youthful affection. He felt the same way about me, but a third party intervened. She was a mutual friend who used to carry messages between us as they attended the same college. I noticed her growing closeness to him, sensing his attention becoming divided. So, I made the difficult decision to let him go. While our budding romance held promise, it lacked the foundation of trust. As a result, it didn't inspire the confidence I needed. This experience influenced me to maintain a distance from the many suitors I encountered, preferring instead to focus on friendships and my career."

Ima continued her story, "I had a dear friend named Sobita, and our bond was a precious one. I met her through a mutual acquaintance. Sobita faced hardship early in life, losing her father at a young age. Raised by her uncle, she had a strong work ethic but struggled financially, especially for her higher education. After passing her Board examination, she aspired to continue her studies but struggled to pay the admission fees. Seeking help, she approached me to use my loom for weaving. Moved by her situation, I agreed, and we began working together.

"We wove *maslai mateks*, cotton stoles with Moirang *pheejin* motifs, which were highly sought after at the time, earning a substantial profit of Rs 50—an impressive amount back then. Our friendship flourished as we worked side by side, often confiding in each other about our personal struggles. With the earnings from our weaving, Sobita managed to fund her education and completed her graduation. Thereafter, she got selected for two jobs, opting for a position at the Regional Tasar Research Station under the Central Silk Board of India, despite also being selected for a government office in Manipur. After I got married, our meetings became less frequent, but we always stayed in touch."

Ima's friendship with Aunt Sobita lasted all her life. Even in their old age, the two made efforts to spend time together. Aunt Sobita visited our home whenever possible, teaching *Ima* yoga, various exercises, and sharing health tips. She also taught us the importance of a balanced diet, nutrition, and regular exercise.

Interrupting *Ima*'s story, I eagerly asked her to describe how she met our father. She smiled warmly and began, "Many proposals for arranged marriages came my way from a young age, but I declined them all. Your father's proposal came through his eldest sister Tolen, your only paternal aunt."

Ima paused thoughtfully, reminiscing about that particular day, and then continued, "I was embroidering a pillow cover on *Inama* Imosakhi's front porch. She was my neighbour. I was wearing a multi-coloured, full-sleeved, round-necked blouse paired with a *hanggam maru pokhaibi* (mustard yellow) *phanek*, with a blood-red Moirang *pheejin* border. My long black tresses were braided and draped over my shoulder. Sitting on a *kouna* mat, I was deeply engrossed in my embroidery work.

"Tolen, in search of a bride for her brother, coincidentally visited my neighbour and took an instant liking to me. Following this, family members started visiting me frequently, armed with gifts. Eventually, they formally proposed marriage and sought my hand for your father, then an assistant sub-inspector (ASI) in the Manipur Police. My parents supported the match and urged me to prepare for marriage. A meeting was arranged, but initially, I declined to meet your father.

"After careful consideration, I eventually accepted the proposal. I felt meeting him was unnecessary, as I was reassured by his education and service in the government's police department, believing him to be capable and sensible person. I resigned myself to fate. At that stage, we exchanged only our photographs."

My father and *Ima* first met each other on their wedding day. *Ima* was 23 years old, which was considered late for marriage in those days. When I saw a photograph of her from that time, I noticed she was tall and slim, with slightly slanting eyes and a strong jawline, reflecting her typical Meitei-Mongoloid features.

My childhood memories of her are of a fair complexion, twinkling almond brown eyes, and a gentle smile. Her long, black, wavy hair was usually styled in a low chignon. She adorned herself in traditional Meitei attire such as the Meitei *phanek*—a traditional wrap around skirt for Manipuri women—and *inaphees* with Moirang *pheejin mayeks*,[2] traditional cotton drapes woven in various colours and designs. Whether she wore a starched Moirang *phee,* a half-saree, or an *inaphee,* paired with a plain *phanek* or a striped *mayek naibi phanek* with bordered motifs, she always carried herself elegantly. She looked exceptionally graceful in our Meitei traditional attire.

---

2 An *inaphee* is a lady's stole, while *pheejin* refers to a designed border. Almost transparent in appearance, *the* Moirang *phee* is a traditional Manipuri stole adorned with extra weft floral patterns. In Meiteilon, the Manipuri language, *phee* means cloth. Moirang is the name of a place in Manipur. A Moirang *phee* has characteristic triangular designs woven along its borders. These triangles are inspired by the sharp teeth of Pakhangba, the serpentine Dragon God of Meitei mythology.

2

A Resolution

The traditional handloom weaving skills in Manipur have been passed down through generations, embodying the state's cultural heritage and reflecting a legacy of exceptional craftsmanship. Primarily transferred from mothers to daughters, these weaving skills have been nurtured and preserved by Manipuri women since time immemorial. In accordance with Meitei customs, a loom used to be included in a girl's *awunpot* or trousseau given by her parents—a practice still observed in many families where weaving is a means of livelihood.

Weaving has always been and continues to be a way of life for Manipuri women. Across both the hills and valleys, they skilfully create a wide range of traditional items including shawls, attire, stoles, scarves, *phanek*s, towels, dress materials, bedsheets, *khudei*s, blankets, mufflers, and sarees, and more. Their deft fingers weave fabrics adorned with intricate patterns, motifs, and vibrant colours, showcasing their artistic prowess. This traditional occupation not only preserves cultural heritage but also provides livelihoods for thousands of people across the state.

Over time, traditional weaving households in Manipur have evolved into clusters or groups, where families weave together in large concentrated hubs of handloom production. Presently, there are numerous handloom clusters under Cluster Development Projects within the National Handloom Development Programme. Manipur boasts the highest concentration of handloom weavers in India, as documented in the National Handloom Census Report, 2010. According to the All India Handloom Census for 2019–20, Manipur is home to 2.12 lakh weavers. Today, handloom weaving is one of the highest income-generating occupations of the state and handloom weavers, mainly women, are the backbone of Manipur's textile industry.

In this multicultural state, each community showcases unique handloom products featuring distinct indigenous and vibrant weft-woven designs. Exclusive motifs are reserved for royalty, while others symbolise special rituals and ceremonies unique to each community. The designs and motifs found in Manipuri handlooms signify a wide array of concepts and symbols.

For instance, the *shaphee lanphee,* a traditional shawl, was bestowed by kings upon brave soldiers as a reward. This shawl displays various shapes and patterns depicting animals like s*hamu* (an elephant), *shagol* (a horse), *iroichi* (a buffalo horn), *nga* (a fish), *numit* (the sun), *tha* (the moon), *thawanmichak* (the star), *phantup* (a seat), *ta* (a spear), and *wahong* (a peacock), intricately woven and embroidered.

Then, there is the Moirang *pheejin*, woven into Moirang *phee* fabric, featuring a distinctive triangular pattern inspired by the serrated teeth of Pakhangba, the serpentine Dragon God of Meitei mythology.

The varied designs in Manipuri handlooms range from floral and animal patterns to shapes of feathers, swords, spears, arrows, bottles (*likli* motifs), diamonds, and more. These designs cater to various occasions, from everyday garments to ceremonial attire and even flags.

Silk fabrics like the Khurkhul *muga phee* and *phanek* are woven from indigenous silk in Khurkhul village, Imphal West district, while the Wangkhei *phee* is a white cotton fabric with local designs and motifs, mostly woven in the Wangkhei area of Imphal East. In the valley region, different *phanek*s and *phee*s are crafted, including those made from Rani silk and *maslai* cotton *phee* in Imphal.

The Meiteis mainly use flying shuttle looms for weaving textiles. Shuttle loom weaving is prevalent across districts such as Imphal East, Imphal West, Bishnupur, Chandel, Churachandpur, Kangpokpi, Senapati, Tengoupal, and Ukhrul in Manipur. This type of loom is also used to weave fishnets using synthetic nylon yarn—these nets are crucial for daily fishing activities in and around the Loktak Lake, Bishnupur district, thereby providing them with a livelihood. In contrast, backstrap loom (also known as loin or body-tension loom) weaving is popular in the hill region and represents one of the oldest methods of cloth weaving. Textiles woven on the backstrap loom are extensively produced in districts like Chandel, Churachandpur, Imphal East, Kamjong, Kangpokpi, Noney, Pherzawl, Senapati, Tamenglong, Tengoupal, and Ukhrul.

Handloom products from the hill districts of Manipur include traditional shawls that uniquely represent each community. Each tribe boasts its distinctive designs and motifs. For instance,

- *Awamphi* are worn by men of the Chothe tribe;
- *Haora*s are large shawls for Tangkhul men;
- *Zosasas* are notable white shawls of the Mao tribe;

- *Pheingao pheisoi*s featuring wide red bands bordered by small yellow, green, and black bands are made by the Kabui tribe;
- *Rengam* of the Chothe tribe adorned with rhombus designs;
- *Thonipui laikot phaizol*s are white shawls worn by Kharam males;
- *Amthal*s are big shawls used by Aimol tribe males;
- *Langampeens are* used by Moyon-Monsang tribes; and
- *Doupuon*s are black shawls worn by both males and females of the Hmar tribe.

These examples represent only a fraction of the diverse range of shawls crafted by different tribes in the region; I have not included many more varieties existing beyond those listed here due to space constraints.

Weaving has been regarded as a symbol of status for women in Manipur. The royal chronicle *Cheitharol Kumbaba* highlights weaving and embroidery as ancient traditional skills and arts of the erstwhile Meitei kingdom. Silk weaving flourished during various reigns of Manipuri kings in earlier times. According to Meitei mythology, the goddess Panthoibi learnt the art of weaving by observing a spider spin its web.

Women who engage in weaving are economically independent, and this inspired *Ima*, who began working on handlooms with the aspiration of achieving financial self-reliance.

Ima continued her story one evening as we sat together after dinner. "Everyone who saw my woven silk saree admired its fine quality, both in texture and design. However, in the beginning, I had few savings and couldn't afford miscellaneous expenses.

"So, I began diversifying my loom products. I started making *pheijom matup*s for men, *maslai matek*s for ladies' stoles featuring

Moirang *pheejin* motifs and various types of *inaphees* and shawls. Alongside weaving on the handloom, I also embroidered bedsheets and pillow covers, ensuring I never wasted time. My embroidery included different flower patterns, designs of swans, roses, China roses, and lotus motifs. Embroidery became more of a hobby for my personal use and collection.

"During my days of struggle when I was weaving various *phee*s, selling the woven clothes was a challenge. Then, a lady named Ebeyaima from our locality (her maternal home was at Yaiskul) who worked at the municipality office saw my creations. She admired the fine stoles, drapes, and fabric varieties, and recognized the effort I put in. Ebeyaima provided substantial support by taking my handloom products to sell at her workplace. Moreover, she assisted me in getting an interest-free loan, which I managed to repay before my marriage.

"I am deeply grateful to her for all the assistance she provided. Soon, I started saving money from the profits generated by diversifying my handloom clothes and increasing sales. This enabled me to contribute to family expenses as well as increase my personal savings. It was with these savings that I could cover most of the expenses for my wedding. Planning for a daughter's wedding is always a huge responsibility and a cause for concern regarding finances. But my earnings allowed me to contribute to the wedding expenses.

"With my hard work and savings, I managed to acquire my own jewellery—gold earrings and gold necklaces. I could buy all the essential *uppu kangdhon*—furniture, beds, and cupboards crafted from the finest wood, including that of Manipur's state tree, the *Uningthou* or Tree King (*Phoebe hainesiana*). In addition, I gathered various other necessary accessories, both major and minor, required for a wedding. I also had my collection of *inaphee*s and *mayek naibi phanek*s. It brought me great joy to be able to finance most of the bridal trousseau myself, and I felt content knowing I did not burden my family during my wedding.

"Even though I was born in a poor family, I never felt discouraged. I turned to my skills in weaving and embroidery, which became my passion. I immersed myself completely in weaving. But one thing that hurt me very early in my life was the breakup of our close-knit family. It was a turning point in my life. My parents endured whatever came in their life, including the different attitudes of their children. Yet, I couldn't bear unkind words that wounded my self-esteem.

"The disintegration of our family strengthened my resolve to work harder and stand on my own feet. I never believed in being weak, feeling helpless, and relying on others. I believed in the power of hard work and my ability to weave. I sought a life of dignity, distancing myself from the mindset and lifestyle I observed, where many wasted their talents and time, lamenting their birth into poverty instead of striving to change their circumstances. I struggled to be independent and eagerly took on responsibilities from a young age.

"I was born and raised in my parents' home, and I was content there. I have neither complaints nor sadness about my unfulfilled wishes. I am grateful every day, in every way. My parents have put their best efforts into raising me and my siblings. I strongly felt blessed with life and understood I had to work to achieve my goals—a resolve I've carried throughout my life. I saw people failing to bring positive changes in their circumstances. The more I saw them, the more it became clear to me that what I wanted was to live with dignity.

"I knew deep down that I had a choice to make: either to give up and moan about my fate of being born in a poor family or to make a difference in my life by working hard and changing its course. While we cannot dictate our birth circumstances or what life brings to us, we always have a choice to make positive decisions and move forward with determination."

Ima looked up, her eyes gleaming behind her brown-framed spectacles. "Well, that's enough for today. Come and help me with my stitching," she said, picking up the needle of her *leiroom*. I held the *leiroom* steady as she skilfully sewed the two halves of her woollen shawl together.

3

Sleep a Bit, Eat a Bit (*Tumba Machet, Chaba Machet*)

Ima, a *Kshetrimayum ningol*, married our father, who belonged to the Oinam family in Sagolband, Sayang Konthoujam Leikai, Imphal West, guided by her belief in destiny. (In Manipur, we don't have a caste system. For Meitei community, lineage is traced through seven clans, each with a specific surname; the Oinams belong to the Khuman clan).

Our father's name was Daoji Oinam, but we affectionately called him *Baba*. Born on 25 November 1945, he was the youngest of four siblings. His sister was called Paonam *Ongbi* Tolen and his two brothers, Oinam Achou and Oinam Gokul. Despite losing his parents early in life, Baba was cared for by his elder siblings. Aunt Tolen often reminisced that *Baba* was an obedient child who eagerly helped her and his brothers with household chores.

Through hard work and determination, *Baba* got a position as an assistant sub-inspector (ASI) in the Manipur Police Department.

Tall and well-built, he was known for his integrity, kindness, and his journey as a self-made man. He had a deep love for reading.

When *Ima* got married to *Baba*, they initially lived together with his brother Oinam Gokul, as his eldest brother Oinam Achou had already moved out to a separate house. As *Ima* recalled about her early days of marriage, I continued jotting down her words.

"The first time I went to the kitchen to make tea in my new home, I felt totally lost. I found only sugar and tea leaves and was unable to locate ginger and bay leaves, which I considered essential ingredients for tea. This marked the beginning of numerous minor differences between my maternal home and my new home. In other words, there was a total shift of life from my maternal home, requiring adjustments in every small detail with my new family. It made me realize how distinct two families can be in terms of behaviour, customs, cooking, beliefs, and lifestyle, each uniquely that of a small niche.

"All my time was consumed by tending to the needs of our joint family, keeping the house clean, cooking, husking rice, and managing all other household chores. Back then, there was no rice mill, so I had to manually separate the rice from the husks using a *chakri* to grind the paddy. After grinding, I would pound it with a wooden *shuk*, which looked like a big pestle, handful by handful in a *shumban,* a wooden device that resembles a big mortar. This process had to be repeated until all the husks were removed from the rice grains.

"Life today is much easier in many ways. In those days, everything had to be done manually at home. The pounding was a continuous effort, made easier when my sister-in-law joined me. Yet, the pounding was only the beginning; using a *yangkok,* we would winnow the rice chaff to further separate the husks from the rice grains. The whole process was time-consuming and exhausting. But whatever the situation was, I was happy and endured any disagreements. With time, I gradually learnt the preferences of my new family.

"In the early days of our marriage, your father was stationed in Jiribam, a town quite far away from Imphal. At that time, Jiribam was part of the Imphal East district. It was declared a separate district only in 2016. Kemila was born a year after we married. As time passed, your father and I felt the need to establish our own household, especially since his parents had passed away early in his life. We realised we needed to live independently and take charge of all responsibilities. However, his savings weren't sufficient to finance a new home, so I sold my gold jewellery to raise funds.

"Oinam Kabi, your father's cousin, helped us to build our house. He was familiar with *Meitei Yumsharol*, a guidebook on traditional Meitei house construction. A beloved brother to your father, he was always there to help us, whether it was building or renovating our house, digging a pit, constructing our granary, or offering guidance on astrological charts. He had a deep knowledge of *kundali*s and could read these birth charts. It was because of him that we could swiftly shift to our own modest dwelling—a simple *kucha* structure with galvanised steel roofing."

We used to affectionately call *Baba*'s cousin *Ipal* Kabi. Whenever he visited us, he delighted us with humorous anecdotes and captivating historical tales. A master storyteller, he was a professional reciter of the *Mahabharata*. He recounted his experiences during the Japanese air raids[1] in Imphal during the Second World War, when

1 Japanese soldiers fought against the British forces at Maibam Lotpa Ching, also known as the Red Hill, during the Battle of Imphal, a significant engagement in Second World War. Today, the India Peace Memorial at Maibam Lotpa Ching is a much-visited site in Manipur, often regarded as a place of pilgrimage, particularly for Japanese tourists.

he was just a young boy. We listened eagerly as he vividly described the sirens blaring to warn of approaching Japanese aircraft, the occasional bombings, and how he and others sought refuge in pits and makeshift trenches for shelters. He would often chuckle, noting that even *Baba* had not yet been born during those tumultuous times.

Coming back to *Ima*'s narration, I vividly recall her story: "Your father used to take me to his quarters in Jiribam by flight. One particularly harrowing journey I will never forget was from Imphal to Silchar. Due to bad weather conditions, our flight was diverted from Imphal to Guwahati since landing at Silchar was not possible. The plane encountered severe turbulence for about three hours, shaking violently. At one point, it became so dark that I, along with all the other passengers, felt immense fear. Finally, after what seemed like an eternity, we safely landed in Guwahati, much to our relief. To compensate for the ordeal, the airline arranged rooms for us at a five-star hotel and bore all expenses. At the hotel, your father was concerned that I might struggle with the cutlery and table manners, but I managed by observing and following his lead—later, he admitted his unnecessary worry. We were served tea in our room, had lunch, went for an outing and shopping at Guwahati Bazaar, and then had dinner.

"The next morning, we flew to Silchar, but after that terrifying experience, I never quite felt comfortable on flights. From Silchar, we travelled to Jiribam by road in a taxi. The weather in Jiribam was scorching hot with high humidity, but I was relieved to be back on solid ground.

"Another chilling incident happened when your father was stationed at Mayang Imphal. I was staying in the quarters with Kemila, who was a toddler of around one year old at the time. The backyard of the Mayang Imphal police quarters where we stayed was swampy, with tall, unkempt grass and huge trees. Behind this marshy area lay a jungle, which I found quite frightening, knowing it home to reptiles and wild animals.

"The quarters adjacent to ours was occupied by a havildar's family. One day, I heard the havildar's wife scream in terror, 'Tiger! There's a tiger in the backyard!' Thinking the tiger might be approaching my kitchen, I grabbed your sister and Debeshor, Aunt Tolen's son who was staying with us that day, and rushed to the havildar's quarters. Your father was at the police station, so we anxiously waited at the havildar's quarters until he returned.

"The next morning, we found large tiger paw marks between our quarters and the havildar's. I couldn't shake off the fear for the remainder of our stay at the Mayang Imphal police quarters, especially since Kemila was so young and vulnerable.

"Your father used to leave early in the morning around 6.a.m. and return late at night, cycling to his police station. I would wash his bicycle in the early morning. Sometimes he would come home for lunch if he had the time. We always had dinner together, but he would often go to Imphal to buy milk and would be gone for a long time. It was challenging for me to pacify your sister as she would cry, and I would worry about his safety until he returned. Fear would often grip my heart in the middle of the night when I was alone in the quarters.

"Usually, he would lock the door from the outside when he left for work, leaving me inside. However, he often returned very late due to his busy schedule. During these times, I felt idle and scared of staying alone in that place. I had always been used to weaving and working, so being unoccupied was uncomfortable for me. I felt it was not right to waste time. Eventually, I made up my mind not to stay at the quarters where your father was posted.

"Due to his active duty, your father stayed at the police station quarters where he was assigned. Since I had moved back to our house in Imphal, I had to take charge of everything at home in his absence, managing the household and shouldering all responsibilities single-handedly. At times, it felt like a one-person struggle. Even during my pregnancy, I pounded rice grains in the *shumban* with the *shuk*, mopped the mud floor, fetched water from the common pipeline or our pond, and attended to all other daily chores. It was overwhelming, and I broke down emotionally many times. However, I knew I had to be strong and resilient in embracing motherhood.

"During my pregnancies, your father was always supportive and helped with necessary preparations. He would buy charcoal bags and leave them at home for me. The charcoal was used after the baby was born to keep the room warm and also to heat my lower back, which eased my back pain. He also made sure fresh fish[2] was stocked in aluminium pots for me. I ensured everything was ready: all the *ningdha*s washed, and the nearby midwife informed in advance.

"I would call my mother, my sister-in-law Jamini (my eldest brother's wife), and her daughter Indira. Nolini and Mota, your aunt Ekashini's daughters, used to accompany Indira to keep me company and assist after the delivery. They were young girls then, and I directed them from my bed as they ran around fetching whatever I needed. However, they could only stay for a short time, as they had their own

---

2 After childbirth, a Meitei woman mainly eats a diet centred on rice accompanied by smoked fish, *hentak* (a thick fermented paste made from dried fish and *hongu, Colocasia esculenta*), and traditional salt cakes made from salt sourced from Manipur's salt wells. Curries are prepared without oil for at least 45 days following delivery as part of the traditional postpartum dietary practices.

responsibilities to tend to back home. I did not have enough time to rest even if I wanted to and could not take care of my health after giving birth. Using a *nahong* as a baby sling, I managed household chores with the baby on my back.

"After Kemila, Robert was born, followed by four more of you with age gaps of about two to three years. Kemila was the only one born in a hospital; the rest of you came into the world at home with the help of a midwife."

I still remember my sisters telling me that they went to school in the morning and returned home to find a new baby in the house—that baby was me! After going through labour pains and giving birth, a woman needs rest for proper physical and mental recovery. Unknowingly, *Ima* risked her life each time she gave birth at home, without thinking about the various complications that a woman might face during labour without an institutional delivery, when doctors and nurses are there to take charge. Fortunately, she did not face complications, but she did not have the luxury of rest either. She had to cook and clean, while carrying me on her back and caring for her other children, often neglecting her own physical and mental needs. Her own health and well-being took a backseat to the needs of our family. *Ima* selflessly looked after us without sparing herself.

Recalling those early days of motherhood, *Ima* said, "Becoming a mother is both a blessing and a hardship, especially when you were all very young. I did not have time to do other things. There's a Manipuri phrase meant for young mothers, '*Tumba machet, chaba machet*', which means 'Sleep a bit, eat a bit'—it perfectly describes the life of a young mother like me. My sleep was always interrupted by a crying baby at night, and I rarely had the luxury of eating a proper meal. I would steal naps whenever you all slept, whether it was during the day or night. I would eat after feeding you all. Even while eating, I had to attend to your unscheduled needs, like comforting a crying child and cleaning up after them during meals.

"I had to make sure that you all stayed safe as you crawled and later walked around the house, trying to climb on furniture. I had to be vigilant, watching every move you made. When you grew older, I had to finish my chores quickly to ensure your study schedules at home and school were met on time. I had absolutely no time to relax. I tried to complete my household chores during your nap times, early in the mornings, and sometimes late at night after putting you all to bed. There were moments when my shoulders ached, my arms and legs felt numb, and all I craved was a good sleep.

"Physically and emotionally, it was exhausting and challenging. There was no one else to rely on; I felt isolated at times. Even if I wanted to socialise with relatives, friends, or neighbours, there was no time. The older children were already attending school when you, *Bem*, were born. Each of your needs was different, and the tasks to be done were never-ending" (I was called *Bem* at home although my real name is Sonia.)

"Nevertheless, I made an effort to attend social ceremonies and events held in our locality or by our relatives, especially since your father was often occupied with work or stationed outside Imphal and couldn't attend. Every invitation to our family held social significance, so I saw it as an opportunity to engage with our community and relatives, showing goodwill. I am grateful to Bamon Sushila, Yaikhom Memtombi, and the other weavers who worked with me at home by looking after all of you whenever I had to attend such occasions.

"I always felt overwhelmed and anxious when any of you fell sick, particularly when your father was not around. I took great care to prevent illnesses. When one of you fell sick, it often spread because you were constantly in close contact—eating, sleeping, and playing together. I mostly relied on local medicinal plants like *leipungkhanga* (fruits of *Solanum* sp.) and *nongmangkha* leaves (*Phlogocanthus sp.)* to prepare traditional remedies for fevers, colds, and coughs. Fortunately, minor ailments got better with these traditional treatments. Whenever one of you had a cold or fever, I would give boiled *nongmangkha* to all of you as a precaution."

Her narration was momentarily interrupted as we both burst out laughing when I recalled how *Ima* would give me boiled *nongmangkha* whenever my siblings fell sick even if I wasn't sick myself! It was a bitter medicine, but effective at warding off infections. *Phlogocanthus* leaves are a staple in Manipuri households to keep colds and flu at bay: a sip of the boiled leaves or inhaling their steam is a quick remedy for colds, coughs and runny noses.

When any of us was sick, *Ima* stayed by our side, gently sponging us with a soft cotton cloth until the fever subsided. Alongside prescribed medicines, she applied her homemade mixture of kerosene, edible oil, and camphor to each child's forehead, neck, navel, palms, and soles. When fever and cold left us with a bitter taste and no appetite, she would buy *kabok aphaba* (puffed rice), which was so bland that we didn't mind eating it. Once we started feeling a bit better and our appetite returned, she would prepare our favourite spicy potato curry. After straining the excess water from the rice cooked over a very low flame, she made us drink the boiled rice water known as *chabon*. Seasoned lightly with salt to make *chabon* tasty, we enjoyed sipping it.

Ima continued, "When you were all young and during my struggles as a mother, I couldn't arrange the customary Meitei social ceremonies and rituals that are usually celebrated with great fanfare by every family.[3] These rituals include *ipalthaba*, the celebration and rituals performed soon after a baby is born; *chakumba*, the first feeding of solid food to a baby after four to five months; *nahut nareng*, the ear-piercing ceremony and the first haircut after birth; and *laiming louba*, the coming-of-age ceremony marking the adulthood and eligibility of young girls for marriage. We conducted ceremonies simply at home without inviting friends and relatives. Usually, a priest performs prayers for young girls during the *laiming louba*, but for the four of you, *Baba* chanted the prayers and conducted the ritual at home."

A typical day for *Ima* began at dawn around 4.30 a.m. After sweeping and cleaning the house, she bathed and performed morning prayers. She meticulously scrubbed the brass plates, pots, and incense stick stands with ashes until they sparkled. She always offered prayers to Lainingthou Sanamahi, the supreme deity and guardian of the Meiteis, Leimarel Ima Sidabi, the supreme goddess in Sanamahism, and Surya Dev, the sun god, using incense sticks, burning candles, *takhellei* (ginger lily), and other flowers on the brass plate. Afterward, she prepared our tea and snacks. While we studied, she fetched tap water from the common pipeline and began cooking our morning meal so that it was ready by 7.30 a.m. to match our school schedule.

We always ate steaming rice accompanied by her delicious curries, with fish curry being her speciality. She prepared all the traditional

---

3 In Meitei tradition, every significant event in a person's life, from birth to death, is marked by specific occasions and rituals, celebrated in a grand manner. Following these rituals, there is a luncheon called *chakkouba* or *ushop*, where people from the locality, along with friends and family, are invited to join in the festivities.

Manipuri dishes such as *chagempomba* (a curry prepared from fermented soyabean), *peas ooti* (peas cooked with a bit of cooking soda), *paknam* (a spicy baked dish made from besan flour), *eromba* (a curry of boiled potatoes, fermented fish, chillies, and vegetables), *kangshoi* (a vegetable stew), *kangmet* (mashed potatoes with roasted chillies), *kanghou* (stir-fried vegetables), and *ngarel* (a fish curry). We savoured every bite she prepared.

After dressing us in our school uniforms, she would gently sniff our foreheads, a Meitei tradition believed to offer protection against evil forces, before sending us off to school. Once we were on our way, she would complete the remaining household chores. Using a polang, a woven bamboo basket, she carried utensils to the edge of our pond where she washed them. On Sundays and holidays, *Ima* washed all our clothes for the week, including our school uniforms and *Baba*'s office wear, as there was no washing machine at our house.

Afterward, she would sit on our front porch, releasing her chignon to let her wet, long, black, wavy hair dry in the sunlight while enjoying her morning meal. Her hair always carried a soothing fragrance of *chenghi*, rice water boiled with aromatic herbs like *khongjainapi* (*Ageratum conyzoides sp*), *tera paibi* (*Gynura cusimbua sp.*), and *yempat* (*Plantago major sp.*), among others. We often gathered these herbs from our backyard or nearby playground. Once her hair was dry, she would prepare to weave on her loom.

Whenever *Baba* stayed home, he used to drop us younger sisters to school in the morning on his blue Bajaj scooter (Kemila and my brothers went to school on their bicycles, while Promila and Dhanabati usually walked or boarded a rickshaw until their seventh or eight grade when they were ready to go to school by bicycle). *Ima* would come to pick us up from school, walking from our home through Mayaikoibi, taking the shorter route. When I was very young, she would carry me on her back as she walked. We sisters studied at Little Flower School, which was about 4 km away from our house.

After we returned from school and played, *Ima* would continue with her daily tasks: weaving, starching the mosquito nets, husking and winnowing rice, tending to her kitchen garden, preparing dinner, and sweeping the house before evening prayers. Once her household chores were completed, she visited her weavers' homes to collect the mosquito nets they had made. Returning home, she performed her evening prayers and then urged us to stop playing so that we could study before dinner and continue afterward. While we studied, *Ima* sat beside us, spinning yarn in her *tareng* until we finished around 8.30 p.m. to 9 p.m. She insisted on early bedtime so that we could wake up punctually for school. She would retire to bed after finishing her spinning.

Ima loved to watch Hindi films although she did not have much time to watch television. We were allowed to watch TV programmes only on selected days of the week like *Chitrahaar* on Wednesdays and *Ek Se Badkar Ek* on Saturdays, both musical shows featuring Bollywood songs, on Doordarshan (DD) National and Doordarshan (DD) Metro. Other channels were not available. Sundays were more relaxed, and we could watch TV freely, including Hindi films at 4 p.m. on DD National, which *Ima* never missed.

She would purchase locally made milk curd from women who carried small black earthen pots in a *thumok* (a hand-woven traditional bamboo basket). Typically, around 10 to 15 pots would fit in one *thumok*, and during summer, *Ima* selected the best milk curd for us. In winter, she kept us warm with her knitted sweaters, mufflers, and adorable multi-coloured winter capes. To provide additional warmth, she would burn charcoal in a *meiphu* (a portable iron firepit) around which we gathered, enjoying the warmth. Our winter vacations were spent listening to her stories while sitting in a circle around the *meiphu*, munching on roasted potatoes, *u-mangra* (cassava), peas, Indian olives, and other snacks.

Ima's storytelling skills were exceptional; she shared many Manipuri folklores and mythical stories with us, teaching us valuable morals. She also recounted tales from the epics—the *Ramayana* and the *Mahabbharata*—that she had learnt through oral recitations during her own childhood and youth. We cherished everything she taught us, finding it both fascinating and inspiring.

As mentioned earlier, our family followed Sanamahism, the indigenous religion of the Meitei community. In every Meitei household, Lainingthou Sanamahi is worshipped as the house deity, with the southwestern corner of the house dedicated to worship. Through *Ima*'s stories, we learnt about our culture, traditions, and the origin of our indigenous religion. She often narrated the mythical story of Lainingthou Sanamahi to us. Here is a snippet of that story:

Ima told us, "In every Meitei household, it is believed that Lainingthou Sanamahi and Leimarel Sidabi guard us. Guru Atiya Sidaba, the Supreme Eternal Godhead, and Leimarel Sidabi had two sons, Sanamahi and Pakhangba. Sanamahi, the elder brother, possessed great physical strength, while Pakhangba had the unique ability to transform into a serpent. When the time for succession came, the Supreme Godhead gave a difficult task to Sanamahi and Pakhangba: they had to complete seven rounds of the universe, and the victorious one would claim the *phambal* (throne). Confident in his strength, Sanamahi immediately set out to complete the task. Pakhangba, on the other hand, was caught in a dilemma.

"Leimarel Sidabi, aware of her sons' strengths and weaknesses, intervened when she saw the dilemma Pakhangba was facing. She provided him with a crucial hint, suggesting that making seven rounds of their father's *phambal* would be equivalent to circling the entire universe. She explained that the *phambal* referred to the whole universe. Following her guidance, Pakhangba circled his father's *phambal* seven times and thereby claimed it as his own.[4]

"On the other hand, the Supreme Godhead consoled Sanamahi upon his return after completing his task, and praised him for achieving the set aim. As a reward, he appointed Sanamahi to reign as the ruling deity in every household. Pakhangba was granted permission by his father to rule as the deity of the Meitei kingdom. Therefore, Pakhangba, the serpentine Dragon God in Meitei mythology, is not worshipped inside the house, whereas Sanamahi is revered in every Meitei household as the house deity."

To summarise what I admired about *Ima*, she fully embraced motherhood and devoted herself wholeheartedly to fulfilling all her responsibilities. Despite all the hardships she had to face, she made every effort to look after us and our family, ensuring our well-being and health. She took every possible precaution to protect us from illness, spent quality time with us, and imparted valuable knowledge about folklore, myths, religion, and important values that shaped our lives. She was the epitome of what a mother should be.

---

4 Nongda Lairen Pakhangba is recorded as the first historical king of Manipur in AD 33 in the *Cheitharol Kumbaba,* the royal chronicle of the erstwhile Meitei kingdom. Under his leadership (AD 33–154), the Ningthouja dynasty began to flourish, establishing a consistent continuity of rule in Manipur that lasted until the reign of Maharaja Bodhchandra (AD 1941–49).

4

The Initial Struggle

Ima continued her story during our post-dinner conversations on another day, reflecting on the challenges she faced after the birth of six children.

"After you all were born, our family's expenses started increasing day by day. I was finding it hard to manage everything solely on your father's salary of about Rs 3,000 per month. His frequent travels to Delhi for work, though necessary, added to our financial burden. I faced tough times whenever he was away on these official tours or during his long in-service training sessions. To cope with the growing expenses, I started borrowing money from local moneylenders. At one point, I even tried participating in a lottery through agents. I got lucky only twice—Rs 200 on a Rs 5 ticket and Rs 400 on another Rs 5 ticket. Eventually, I stopped when I realized it wasn't a reliable solution.

"There were times when our *chengfu* (a traditional rice pot for storing rice) would be empty. Some days, I couldn't even afford the fare for conveyance and had to walk from our home to my sister Sakhi's house at Singjamei. She supported me generously during those hardships.

"I tried to manage by adopting different strategies. I began taking groceries on credit, ensuring I settled the debt every month when your father received his salary. He was loved and respected by people in our locality, so they trusted us. We had to maintain this trust and were careful never to betray it. Yet, despite these efforts, times remained tough.

"I remember a particular instance during *Imoinu Iratpa* when I couldn't afford to buy fish, which is traditionally offered to Goddess *Imoinu* for prosperity. It was then I realised that I had to do more than just rely on credit and borrowing. With your father's salary as the only source of income for our family, I finally decided to start weaving handloom products with the hope that selling them would help us overcome our financial hardships.

"My mother had included a *kon* (a Manipuri handloom) in my trousseau. Weaving, a skill I had learnt from a young age, became my means to earn and supplement our family income. I resumed weaving various clothes such as *phanek*s, cotton stoles, *khudei*s, *samtu phee matek*s (woollen shawls), bed sheets, mosquito nets, traditional woollen shawls like *haophee tengoupals*. These items were primarily sold during festive seasons like *Ningol Chakkouba*, which is celebrated to strengthen the bond of married women with their families.

"I sold my products locally and also supplied them in bulk to women vendors who traded at *Ima Keithel*. You all were very young and I did not have much time for my weaving. So, I took help of our *leikai leisabi*s (unmarried girls) from our neighbourhood and taught them to weave. I engaged them in my handloom work, particularly for weaving mosquito nets, and paid them for their work.

"I obtained all the necessary yarn from traders at Khwairamband *Ima Keithel* on credit. Initially, a lady named Tomemcha helped me by procuring wool yarn on credit. She acted as the middleman, and the profit made was minimal. I eventually requested her to introduce me directly to Lala, the proprietor of yarns at *Ima Keithel*. There were several prominent *mahajan*s (merchants) who owned large yarn shops there, and over time, I came to know them one by one—Vikas, Indra, Lala, and others.

"Initially, I started by taking credit from Lala for small bundles of yarn—one bundle at first, then two, and eventually three bundles and more—as my sales and weaving network expanded. Indra also reached out to me to purchase yarn from his shop. He provided discounts and extended credit terms, and at times, even accepted starched mosquito nets we produced during off-seasons in exchange for yarn. Later, these starched mosquito nets were sold by these shopkeepers to the mosquito net vendors at *Ima Keithel*.

"One day, while doing routine accounts, a calculator belonging to one of the *mahajans* accidentally ended up in my bag. The next day, I returned it to them, explaining the mistake. They were pleased with my honesty and praised me for it. From then on, there was no looking back. Their trust in me grew significantly. To strengthen this trust further, I introduced your father to these *mahajans*, ensuring they knew I came from a respected family.

"As time went on, their trust and our business dealings grew. Initially, your father was uncertain about my decision to visit Khwairamband *Ima Keithel*. However, he gradually realised that my expertise was driving our business forward and began supporting me wholeheartedly. On his days off, he would help me, even spinning yarn on the spinning wheel late into the night.

"After teaching our *leikai leisabis* to weave mosquito nets, I began building a network of skilled weavers to expand my work. Selecting the right weavers was crucial; many women from nearby areas approached me to weave mosquito nets, but not all could achieve the desired uniformity and thickness in their work. While I initially gave opportunities to many, I eventually had to refine my group of weavers.

"I focused on working with a select group of talented weavers from our *leikai* and also from nearby *leikai*s. They included Bamon Sushila, Bamon Shanti, Yaikhom Memtombi, Soyam Nungshi, Naorem Memcha, and Mutum Yangbi from our neighbourhood, along with Memthoi from Khuraijam, weavers from Sapam *leirak*, Pebam Ebeni, Bino, Bheiga and others from Kuraomakhong, and Yaimabi from Mayaikoibi. Some weavers from Lukram Leirak, like Sana and others, also joined our team. These skilled weavers produced mosquito nets of the required thickness and uniformity. I valued those who completed their work promptly and with quality. However, I had to let go some weavers who did not meet deadlines, realising that timely completion was crucial for maximising earnings. Once the nets were ready, I starched them myself and sold them to women vendors at Khwairamband *Ima Keithel*.

"In this manner, I began my venture of making mosquito nets with a small group of weavers from nearby localities and *leikai leisabi*s from our neighbourhood. The proceeds from selling the starched mosquito nets allowed me to clear all dues to the *mahajan*s and pay my weavers promptly. Gradually, I started earning enough to generate profits. I repaid the borrowed money to the local moneylenders and began saving money by participating in the monthly tender *marups* managed by our community elders. These *marups* were small saving schemes where each participant contributed Rs 200, and almost every family in our locality had one or more shares. The payouts from these *marups* varied from Rs 2,000 to a maximum of Rs 18,000, with the largest sum going to the final participant in line. I did not get the maximum amount from the *marups* because at a time of urgent requirement, I quoted a smaller amount to get the tender.

"With my earnings, I purchased essential food items, groceries, smoked fish for our *ngarubak*, and rice to keep our *chengfu* consistently stocked. This enabled me to boost our family's income and meet our daily expenses more comfortably."

I vividly remember how *Ima* would diligently weave on her *kon*, meticulously starch the mosquito nets, and then go to Khwairamband *Ima Keithel* to sell them. Let me describe these processes elaborately for my dear readers.

It was an intricate process. A *kon* had many components to be set up before weaving. *Ima*'s *kon*, a fly shuttle loom, was placed in our front porch. When selecting a specific fabric for weaving, whether for a mosquito net, *phanek* or bedsheet, the number of cloths in one *eyong* or weave had to be determined first. *Ima* would delegate the spinning of yarns for the extra warp beam, known as *eyong houba*, to another skilled artisan in the nearby locality of Mayaikoibi. This involved winding the warp threads around the extra warp beam until the number of cloths to be woven was finalised. *Ima* would collect the warp beam once the *eyong houba* was completed. The extra warp beam was then installed at the rear of the loom. Adjustments were made by rolling the warp beam and stretching the warps through numerous heddles. The spreading warps were carefully placed by adjusting the warp beams.

She used spindle-shaped wooden weaving shuttles, each of which required small wooden spools called *langchaks* to be loaded inside. These *langchaks* were essential for holding the threads spun from the yarn using a spinning wheel called a *tareng*. The *tareng* has two wooden spinning wheels: a larger wheel on the left and a smaller one on the right with a handle. Before spinning, the yarn purchased from the yarn shops had to be properly starched. *Ima* would wind these starched yarns, known as *langharei,* around the big spinning wheel. Using the handle on the smaller right wheel, she spun the yarn onto the *langchak,* starting by loosely tying a loose end of the starched yarn around the *langchak*. The yarn thread kept winding around the *langchak* from the big left spinning wheel. Before beginning the actual weaving process, *Ima* ensured that several *langchak*s, each loaded with yarn threads, were prepared to weave a certain length of cloth.

These loaded *langchak*s were then placed into the spindle-shaped shuttles of the loom. During weaving, *Ima* used a *singkap* to hold the woven cloth firmly. She initiated the weaving process by manually pulling a sling attached to the loom, which propelled the spindle-shaped shuttle back and forth, weaving the spread across the loom.

Ima slammed the threads with a wooden beam in synchronisation with each throw of the shuttle in a uniform speed as her legs pressed the thin wooden treadles, left and then right alternately. She maintained a perfect coordination of her hands and legs. The shuttle's movement produced a distinctive sound, followed by the rhythmic thud of the wooden beam and the soft movements of her feet on the treadles. The manner in which the sling was pulled and weaving was done determined the cloth's thickness and appearance. *Ima* was an expert at it.

Weaving is an art and she had it in her veins. The time required to weave varied depending on the type of cloth. It took two or three days to weave a full length of a mosquito net, or a day if the weaving was done continuously. Other cloths with shorter lengths required even less time.

During weaving, interruptions were common due to thread breaks. Each interruption required finding the exact point of the broken thread and retying it through the precise heddle position on the loom. Once a certain length of cloth was woven, *Ima* would ease the tension by pulling the cloth towards the weaver's beam. This involved securing the ends of the loom's sword and the woven cloth, which were then rolled up on the warp beam below the loom. All the woven lengths of cloth were rolled onto this warp beam.

My sisters also learnt to weave and helped *Ima* whenever possible. They spun the yarns in the *tareng* and provided *langchak*s for her weaving. Since *Ima* was often occupied with household chores, all the *leikai leisabi*s who worked with her also helped her immensely. *Ima* treated them all as her younger sisters and cherished them like family. They shared a strong bond, supporting each other through personal challenges. *Ima* found a unique way to connect with people in our community, fostering mutual friendships alongside her work. We always considered them part of our family. *Iche* Memtombi, in particular, was a dear sister to all of us. Much older than Kemila, she was slender and of medium height. With a small oval face, she was very pretty. Besides being a skilled weaver, she also took care of us whenever *Ima* was away and always attended to our needs.

The next step after weaving a mosquito net involved starching it with flour. White flour had to be cooked in a large pot and stirred continuously to prevent lumps from forming. We were often given the task of stirring the flour. Once cooked, the flour was poured onto a thick cloth and kneaded thoroughly to extract the fine starch fluid. The amount of the starch was prepared according to the number of nets to be starched. After soaking the nets in the starch fluid for about 15 minutes, *Ima* would then vigorously wring and hurl each net to ensure no excess starch remained—a process that typically required two people to hold, hurl, and stretch the nets for even distribution of starch.

The starched nets were then dried by using *uyung*s, thin wooden poles, in our backyard. About 10 or more mosquito nets were starched in a day. Folding the starched nets properly and neatly required assistance, which the *leikai leisabi*s provided whenever a second person was needed. On Sundays and holidays, we used to help *Ima* with starching and drying the nets.

Ima would then carefully bundle the neatly folded nets into two packages and take them to *Ima Keithel* in a rickshaw. There, she delivered them to women vendors, who collected all such starched mosquito nets from *Ima* and other weavers from different places. These vendors sold the nets after sewing them into usable forms. Sometimes they paid her immediately, but other times she had to collect her money from the vendors on another day.

We eagerly awaited her return from *Ima Keithel* with her big *keithel* bag. As soon as she came home, we would search her bag for locally made snacks like white *bera*s (sweets made of milk), *khurman*, *halwa*, *waatin*, and *rasgula*s. She always carried a small notebook in which she recorded her transactions with weavers and women vendors. This included details such as the amount of yarn supplied, payment requirements for each weaver, the number of nets delivered, the quantity of yarn purchased from shops, and daily credits settled.

Upon returning from *Ima Keithel,* she would ask us to write down her daily transactions in her notebook, which she diligently maintained and updated every day.

While dealing with mosquito nets, *Ima* observed and learnt the skill of sewing them. She purchased a sewing machine and taught us how to stitch the nets, as she was too busy with her weaving and seldom used the sewing machine. In this way, we all learnt weaving, starching the nets, and sewing them.

My sisters began receiving orders to sew mosquito nets from vendors who sold them at *Ima Keithel,* as well as customised orders from individuals. Soon, they were earning their own pocket money.

Later, a person from a nearby locality visited Moreh, a town on the border of India and Myanmar, located in the Tengnoupal district of Manipur. He learnt that there was a huge demand in Moreh for readymade mosquito nets, and upon returning, he shared this information with us. My sisters began accepting orders to sew between 50 and 100 mosquito nets each week. The payment was Rs 5 for a small mosquito net and Rs 10 for a larger-sized one. My elder sisters could sew at least five mosquito nets per day, earning Rs 50 daily. They managed their sewing and weaving activities during their leisure time, balancing them with their study schedules.

Ima assisted my sisters in taking the basic measurements—the length, width, and the *yang* (upper portion) of the mosquito net—and the tailoring cuts were made accordingly. Once these preliminary sketches and cuts were ready, they proceeded with the sewing. All my sisters were skilled weavers. It was extremely difficult to control the sling throw of the shuttle with the right hand, uniformly slamming the thread with the wooden beam using the left hand, and coordinating movements of the left and right feet on the thin wooden treadles of our loom. They were adept at managing all of these tasks simultaneously. Unfortunately, I struggled to learn weaving because I found it difficult to coordinate my hands and legs. However, even though I failed terribly at it, I eventually managed to learn to sew a mosquito net!

Ima would send us to collect mosquito nets from her weavers at their residences. She had engaged around 25 active weavers in our locality as well as nearby areas, including her maternal relatives. While visiting her weavers, we often had the chance to ride our bicycles and explore our nearby neighbourhoods, the roads, and *leirak*s.

Despite her demanding schedule and daily chores, *Ima* continued her hard work and regularly went to Khwairamband *Ima Keithel* to sell her starched mosquito nets. These physically taxing days for *Ima* occurred when we were very young, but they helped alleviate the financial crunch in our family. *Baba* also got subsequent promotions over the years. Through her profits and savings, *Ima* finally purchased a *potpham*, a stall, at *Ima Keithel* in the late 1990s. This *potpham* was dedicated to selling traditional woollen shawls of different varieties such as *haophe*e, *leiroom, lui, kukiphee, khwang, maflar,* and *inaphee*, among others.

Transitioning from her mosquito net business to selling woollen shawls, *Ima* began selling directly from her own *potpham* at *Ima Keithel* instead of supplying them to other vendors. Initially, her daily sales of woollen shawls were highly profitable. Her stall was located at *Laxmi Keithel* (now known as *Emoinu Ima Keithel*), which is quite close to *Shamu makhong* (the statue of Maharaja Bhagyachandra, a revered Meitei monarch of the 18th century known for his martial skills, taming a wild elephant). At that time, the construction of the new *Ima Keithel* had not yet been completed.

Our parents wanted us to study well and never let us feel the brunt of their financial problems. Even as we earned our own pocket money, they encouraged us to manage it wisely for personal expenses and savings. They never took the money we earned, instead motivated us to save it.

Their dedication and hard work not only improved our family's financial stability but also instilled in us the fundamental lesson of industriousness and earning. The money we earned was intended for essential needs, not extravagant spending. They diligently saved through monthly *marup*s, although the amounts were modest, for future use.

Our parents never wasted money unnecessarily and kept reminding us not to do so either. They taught us that in life, survival and success come through hard work and effort, and there is no free meal – everything must be earned.

Ima constantly emphasised, "Always save your money and remember to spend within your means. This will help you to always keep a financial balance."

For *Ima*, work was a source of inner strength. Fully dedicated to weaving, she poured her soul into her craft. The network of weavers she worked with became a two-way support system: she provided guidance and they reciprocated with assistance. Each weaver had responsibilities: supporting their family, educating their children, and overcoming life's hurdles with hard work and skill. *Ima* helped them to develop their weaving abilities. They confided in each other and found emotional strength in their bond. This was more than a fleeting connection; her weavers trusted and collaborated with her as a cohesive team.

Ima established herself as a role model and reliable figure for them, not only guiding them back to work but also opening new avenues. Her dedication to work motivated them to discover a path towards self-empowerment, maximising their time and skills to the fullest extent. Their commitment helped change their lives; some established their own networks after *Ima* moved away from mosquito nets. Many expanded their weaving expertise to create different types of cloth such as *phanek*s, *phee mateks,* shawls, silk stoles, and more. In this way, they achieved financial independence, supporting both their families and themselves.

With sheer willpower and determination, *Ima* overcame the financial hardships our family faced. Through this journey, she not only found a way to connect with our local community but also established friendships that extended beyond. She explored the market at *Ima Keithel,* and forged ties with women vendors, *mahajan*s, and a fresh network of weavers. This marked the beginning of her new venture as a vendor of woollen shawls.

5

Our Family and Lessons Learnt

During his service, *Baba* was stationed at various locations including Mayang Imphal, Khoupum Tampak, Sekmai, Lilong, Imphal City Police, Moreh, and the CID Branch of Imphal, interspersed by in-service training periods outside Manipur. His duties kept him occupied, leaving little time for us. When home, he diligently took on household chores like cleaning the surroundings, strengthening fences, and ploughing the soil to aid *Ima* in growing vegetables. In the backyard, vegetables like potatoes, cauliflowers, chillies, peas, beans, cucumbers, mustard, and tomatoes were laid out in rows. My parents would sprinkle coriander seeds over a patch of freshly ploughed soil and cover them with a wet sack. Tender coriander sprouts would emerge through the sack, fresh and green.

Baba would come home in his khaki uniform, often accompanied by escort personnel in a police jeep. He always carried a heavy pistol on his belt while his escorts had long rifles. We admired how smartly they saluted him, showing their respect. We felt proud of him and always held our heads high knowing our father was a police officer. He served as an inspiration, believing in merit and his own capabilities.

When *Baba* held civil positions, he dressed in a neatly ironed formal suit and carried a briefcase to his office, riding his blue Bajaj scooter. To us, he was the best father. He never spanked us and rarely scolded us. He loved *Ima* and it was obvious that they felt complete with each other. Together, they supported, depended on, and drew strength from one another through the challenges of raising us, pursuing their dreams, and navigating life's ups and downs. They had big hopes and plans for us.

Our home was a semi-*pucca*–semi-*kucha* structure that underwent various transformations over the years. Concrete cement flooring was laid on our *mangol* (front porch) and the middle room, while the other rooms had mud floors. Above the *mangol* window hung a photo frame showcasing the classical *Pung Cholom* dance of Manipur, featuring dancers playing the *Meitei pung*, a percussion musical instrument. And just above our front door was a framed photo of a woman's beautiful hand with long red-painted nails holding red roses, accompanied by the word 'Welcome'. Ima's *kon* and sewing machine were placed in our *mangol*.

On the southern side of the middle room was our parents' room, while the northern front led to two additional rooms occupied by my eldest sister and brother. At the rear of the middle room, there was a room designated for my other sisters. I usually stayed in my parents' room, primarily with my mother since my father often had duties at the police quarters. There was a granary in the southern corner of my sisters' room. Each of our rooms was furnished with a cupboard, a bed and a study table where we kept our exercise books and textbooks.

The last room in our home was the kitchen, a traditional Meitei kitchen. It featured a *leirang*, a traditional earthen oven (mud stove) for cooking with firewood. Over time, as modern amenities became available, we also had a gas cylinder for our gas stoves. Like other Meitei kitchens, ours was equipped with a *chengfu* for rice storage, a *ngarubak* for smoked fish, a *samuk* (brass stand) for keeping cooked food and different *polong*s (bamboo baskets) to keep utensils, vegetables, and other items.

I vividly remember every heavy rainfall, the sound of raindrops on our galvanised steel roof amplified to a tremendous pounding. When hailstones struck, the noise was so deafening that our ears would go numb. We turned it into a game, covering and uncovering our ears in sync with the rhythm of the falling hailstones. Even if we shouted, we could not hear each other unless we screamed at the top of our lungs.

Once, during a fierce nighttime rainstorm with howling winds and thunder, a section of the roofing above our kitchen was blown away. Thankfully, it got repaired the next day.

During thunderstorms, ripe mangoes would fall to the ground, and we eagerly gathered them after the rain subsided. Our *ingkhol* (the surrounding area of our house and uncles' houses), had numerous large trees, including mango, Indian pomelo, olive, guava, peach, lemon, pear, pomegranate, and others that bore fruit. There was a pond on the eastern side of our *ingkhol,* encircled by flowering plum trees, creating a picturesque scene of blossoms and greenery.

At our gate stood a majestic *gulmohar* tree, its branches providing ample shade where we often relaxed or played. The *gulmohar* flowers were orange in colour. Its towering height made it visible from afar, even from Mayaikoibi. Returning home from Little Flower School through Mayaikoibi, the sight of our beloved *gulmohar* tree would brighten our faces, making us feel happy to come back to our home.

To the west of our *ingkhol,* the bamboos grew tall and green, their stems thick and sturdy. Our backyard, filled with green vegetation, became our favourite playground, especially for games like hide-and-seek. Surrounded by such abundant greenery, our home became a tranquil sanctuary.

Baba and *Ima* instilled values in us that we have embraced deeply. They taught us compassion for all—be it our fellow beings, siblings, relatives, or friends. Honesty and sincerity in relationships were principles they upheld and passed on to us. *Baba* had collected books on spirituality which I read during my school and college days—they enriched my spiritual growth. His commitment to duty inspired us to surpass boundaries and persevere in achieving our goals.

Ima, on the other hand, taught us self-reliance and the importance of helping others. She never pressurised us regarding our academic performance; instead, stressed the significance of discipline. She gave us freedom to socialise with friends, yet ensured we maintained our boundaries. Our brothers never stayed out late at night. Above all, she raised us to appreciate simplicity, encouraging us to embody grace and uphold values as we grew into adulthood.

When *Baba* brought home the first Beltek colour television in our *leikai,* our neighbours and fellow residents hurried to our house to watch it. They gathered on our front porch to watch the *Mahabharata* series on Sundays. On occasions when our aunt Tolen visited, we sometimes became absorbed in playing or watching television rather than talking to her. *Baba* was disappointed with our behaviour and urged us to pay attention when relatives, especially our aunt, came to our house. We realised how he felt and resolved to show our love and attention to our aunt and any other relatives who visited. Similarly, *Baba* always extended help to others. During periods of water scarcity in our *leikai*, he arranged water tanks and trucks to distribute water throughout our locality. He always led us to do the right things.

Sharing a unique love and respect, *Baba* and *Ima* always accepted each other and patiently learnt from each one another. Let me recount an incident narrated by my sister Promila.

One day *Baba* had gone out to Moirang with his friends but had not returned even though it was very late at night. *Ima* woke up Promila, expressing her deep worry. She kept checking the door upon hearing any noise, hoping it was *Baba* returning. They anxiously awaited his arrival and finally, around 2 a.m., they heard the knock on the door. It was a cold winter night, and *Baba* arrived freezing and visibly upset. He went straight to the kitchen and collapsed. *Ima* and my sister quickly rubbed his hands to warm him up and lit the *meiphu* for warmth. *Ima* took care of *Baba,* ensuring he rested, though he could not sleep that night.

In the morning, *Baba* recounted the events to *Ima*. There was an argument between *Baba* and his friends, resulting in them leaving him at Moirang. That night, he had to endure a cold, 40-km walk home. This experience prompted deep self-introspection and brought a great change in him. From that day onwards, *Baba* refrained from frequent outings with his friends, and even the occasional gatherings at our house stopped. Throughout all this, *Ima* had shown remarkable patience with *Baba*. She never encouraged casual drinking or get-togethers, especially at our home, regardless of how infrequent it was. *Baba* sometimes felt that her disapproval distanced him from his friends, but *Ima* was always firm and clear about her stance.

Ima's priority was her children and she wanted to keep us grounded in simplicity. The incident at Moirang made *Baba* realise how his social activities had impacted his family life, causing him to overlook many small but important things. He was thankful to *Ima* for all her patience and courage in dealing with all the hardships she had gone through to keep our family together and for raising us with utmost care. Through their trials, both *Ima* and *Baba* had stood up for each other, becoming pillars of strength in each other's lives.

I remember our childhood as a time of innocence, happiness, enthusiasm, and vivid imagination that coloured our experiences. We were deeply involved in our studies, and during leisure hours, we enjoyed playing games at home. Our parents shielded us from any burdens or worries, ensuring that we had the best possible childhood.

I must share one memorable event at *Baba*'s police quarters during the winter of 1992. I was around eight years old, and had just completed my second grade and was relaxing during the winter vacation. *Damcha* (I affectionately called my brother Tiken *Damcha* (Big Brother), while my parents called him Abungo) was around ten years and *Chemcha* (my sister Dhanabati was *Chemcha* to me and Naopisak to my parents) was around 12 years when we got our first opportunity to visit our father's quarters at the Sekmai police station. Our older siblings, known as Kemila and Robert to our parents, and my sister Promila, referred to as Ebemcha, had more frequent opportunities to visit and stay at Baba's quarters. The three of us younger ones formed a small group within the family and had rarely visited his police quarters before.

During our stay in Sekmai, we gained a deeper understanding of *Baba*'s duties and responsibilities. We had no idea of what an OC (officer-in-charge) was, but we learnt that Baba held this role at the Sekmai police station. As a police inspector and officer-in-charge, everything within the station was under his command and control, and all police personnel reported to him.

As we eagerly anticipated the trip to *Baba*'s quarters, my imagination ran wild with visions of discovering new surroundings. I pictured white-painted walls, rooms lined up in rows, a long hallway, and even white rabbits—quite an unusual expectation indeed! It was the winter of December as we packed all our clothes and essentials.

Ima couldn't help but smile at our excitement, and the best part was that she was also joining us. Over time, she had gained some weight, her once slender face now pleasantly plump. She looked graceful in her half-saree paired with a *mapannaibi phanek*, a featuring horizontal stripes, mostly black with alternating pink or other colours.

Baba came to pick us up in a white Ambassador car, and all six of us—three siblings, *Ima, Baba*, and the driver—fitted well into it.

As we drove through Khwairamband Bazaar, the bustling marketplace seemed like a maze to us. Until then, our world has been as small as a frog's well, with our home as the starting point; other places remained a mystery to us. We gazed out through the car's windows, watching as the sun gradually set and it grew darker and darker outside. We saw shadows of small hills, all black with occasional lights from sparsely scattered shops and houses amidst wide fields. By the time we reached the Sekmai police station, it was already pitch-black around us.

Our excitement reached its peak as we jumped down from the packed car. We saw a passage which led to rooms illuminated by light, and at the entrance stood two guards on duty with their rifles. Initially, we mistook it for *Baba*'s quarters, but as we approached the gate, *Ima* suddenly redirected us along another pathway, leaving us quite disappointed.

Before us stood a row of houses facing north, their outlines faint in the darkness. At the end of this row, facing east, was the larger house that turned out to be *Baba*'s quarters. *Ima* explained that the building we had seen earlier was the police headquarters office.

The first thing we did after entering the residence was to explore the rooms. We found a kitchen, a common room in the middle, and another room as a bedroom. There were front and back porches as well. Despite our weariness from our long journey, excitement kept us awake on our first night there. By morning, refreshed by the lovely winter day, we enjoyed a hearty breakfast of hot tea and *samosas* from a nearby hotel. We felt quite at home in the big rooms, especially with *Ima* and *Baba* close by.

The next day of our stay, after breakfast, *Damcha* went missing. All of us started searching frantically for him. He was *Ima*'s favourite, and her worry was evident as she wondered where he could have wandered off to. By 10 a.m. *Damcha* strolled back quite nonchalantly, unaware of the anxiety he had caused, accompanied by a young man named Nandalal. They had taken a leisurely walk up to Sekmai

Bazaar and the foothills of the town. Nandalal, a robust fellow around 24 or 25 years old, lived in the same complex as he was the younger brother of the second-in-command of the police station. He instantly became *Damcha*'s friend.

Ima didn't scold my brother but calmly reminded him of the importance of informing her or *Baba* about his whereabouts before going out. She also warned us to be cautious around strangers, and reminded us that we were not staying in our own home. At the same time, she wanted us to enjoy our vacation. We were allowed to be on our own as long as we did not cause any trouble.

After that incident, we avoided making friends with strangers and relied on Nandalal to take us to the hills, rivers, and sights around Sekmai. In just a few days, the area became familiar to us, and all the personnel at the police station got to know us. We freely roamed around the station grounds, earning ourselves the nickname "the three musketeers"! We climbed the watchtowers, explored all the rooms, including the operating and wireless rooms, *Baba*'s office, the common room with a television, the kitchen, and the large dormitory where police personnel slept. Between the police headquarters and our quarters, there were huge pine trees, a playground, and even some big dogs too!

We felt liberated, enjoying the freedom to run around the vast green playground under the pine trees, often tumbling into somersaults. We gathered armfuls of pine cones, which we later ignited to create bonfires during the winter evenings. Climbing the hills of Sekmai became our most thrilling adventure. We would struggle to ascend, holding onto any support we could find, and finally reach our destination breathless.

There was a school at the top of the hill, and at the edge of its campus stood a charming small house. What remains vivid in my memory is the presence of a skinny black dog near the exit gate. Although tied to a tree, it would bark incessantly, amusing us as we dashed past. We would climb down the small steps at the edge of the hill into broader ones that connected to the road leading to the bridge over the Sekmai River.

Sundays were special, as we were allowed to watch television in the police station. Our favourite was the animated series about Mowgli, the Jungle Boy, and we were diehard fans of its characters and stories. At other times, we listened to *Baba*'s collections of songs like 'Holiday', 'It Must Have Been Love', 'Cheri Cheri Lady', and popular Bollywood movie songs on the cassette player.

Whenever *Ima* went back home to check on Kemila, Robert, and Promila, we felt her absence keenly. We eagerly awaited her arrival, counting slowly—one to 50, and then one to 100, repeatedly. Every passing mini-bus on the road raised our hopes that *Ima* might step out of one of them. When she finally did arrive, her presence instantly lifted our spirits.

I cherished observing her cook on the kerosene stove, wash dishes, do laundry, and manage household chores. I often played nearby while she worked. When her cooking was over, there used to be an instant quietness all around as the loud hiss of the stove would stop.

There was a school, Nilapadma Higher Secondary School, just opposite the Sekmai police station and inside the school campus, there was a big well. In fact, in Sekmai, almost all houses had a well and a *yongchak* (*Parkia speciosa*) tree. This was a novelty for us as we had never seen a well or a *yongchak* tree, on which aromatic beans grow. These beans are plucked and used as an ingredient of *Yongchak eromba*, a favourite local curry of Manipuris, cooked with fermented fish, chillies, and other vegetables.

Ima and we three siblings used to go the school campus and fetch water, which was crystal clear, from the well. We also loved the Indian pomelos that grew in the backyard of the police station. We used to climb the big pomelo trees and swing on the lower branches like monkeys. *Damcha* would pretend to be a growling tiger and we two sisters would jump from the tree branches and run to save our lives! We would run all the way to the front porch of our quarter and hide inside the makeshift house made by *kouna* mats. Then our game would end and we would all laugh. *Ima* would peel the pomelos for us, after which we sat together and relished the fruits with her.

Ima usually took a short nap after her household chores in the quarters and while she rested, we would go out for a walk up to the small lodge, which functioned as a check post, where one or two policemen were on duty. All the vehicles on the road, mainly trucks, had to stop and each driver had to enter the vehicle numbers in the register and pay a small fee of about Rs 5. After the policemen checked the vehicles, the vehicles were allowed to proceed. These friendly policemen would always give us money to buy snacks, our preference being groundnuts.

One sunny day, we proceeded to the nearby *paan* shops by the roadside to buy our groundnuts. When we reached the crossroads, we were terrified to see a herd of cows with sharp horns suddenly running out from one of the streets towards us. We had to run eastward where a crowd of people stood. *Damcha* ran fast but it was too late for me and *Chemcha*. The ferocious-looking cows were getting too close, so we quickly ran back to the *paan* shop, reached the small rear door, slipped inside and slammed it shut just in time. We narrowly missed their horns! After calming down, we saw the two women of the shop staring at us speechlessly, amazed at our fright. However, I think the cows were not harmless and could have hurt us. They roamed around the shop and went away after some time. We rushed out and couldn't stop laughing at our reaction and remembering the comical faces of those women staring at us. After hearing about the incident, *Ima* restricted us from going out without her and our wild adventures at Sekmai came to an end.

As the cliché goes, good things always come to an end and so did our vacation. After spending nearly two months at *Baba*'s quarters, we had to return to Imphal. On our last day there, we packed, and then wore our formal clothes, complete with socks and shoes, for a family photo session. *Baba* took us out to offer prayers at a temple in Kanglatombi and to the Sekmai River. We also watched a football game where *Baba* was a special invitee.

We came back to Imphal and it took a few days to adjust again just like we did when we first reached Sekmai. For some time, we were fascinated with photographs of *Baba* with a Japanese official team who had visited him at the Sekmai police station. They had presented him with Japanese gadgets and other gifts as a token of their visit. *Baba* brought the Japanese solar calculators, magazines, a Japanese harmonica, origami sets, sweets, and Sakura-Cray-Pas Crayons, for us. These Japanese items became a treasure for us. We would flip through the magazines and look at the photographs of orchards and farms in Japan and elegant Japanese women wearing multi-coloured kimonos. The harmonica became a showpiece because none of us knew how to play it. The origami set contained varied colours in fluorescent shades we had never seen before and we made many shapes and patterns by following the pictorial instructions.

The Sekmai vacation hangover got over, and we were back to our routines at home. *Ima* was a disciplinarian who guided us meticulously from our early childhood. She woke us early each morning, and our first task was to make our beds. She scheduled our study sessions at optimal times—early mornings when our minds were receptive, and in the evenings after our play while she prepared dinner.

Ima emphasised cleanliness, ensuring the house was swept and mopped both in the early morning and before evening prayer. She taught us to maintain the same standards when she was occupied with other tasks. She made us do the same when she was busy with her work. The kitchen was always kept tidy, and she scolded us if we left dishes unwashed. We were quite used to her reprimands as it was her way of teaching us self-reliance and responsibility. Under her guidance, we learnt a multitude of practical skills such as cooking, winnowing rice, sweeping, knitting, weaving, sewing, gardening, and more—preparing us for life beyond our home.

Ima constantly reminded us of the very important principle of not wasting time. She would say, "There is no cure for laziness. If you don't work hard, you won't achieve anything in life. Time is precious—do not waste it."

Despite our different temperaments, all six of us siblings could be mischievous at times. *Ima* wasn't hesitant to discipline us, sometimes resorting to spanking and delivering stern lectures. I remember one incident vividly when I was around 10 years old. I misbehaved, and she tied me to the wooden pole of our front porch with a rope for a while as a punishment.

We were often tempted to venture out and to play in the playground near our house, but the gate where the huge gulmohar tree grew was our boundary, our *Lakshmana Rekha*. *Ima* had restricted us from playing in the local playground or visiting friends' homes too frequently. While we were allowed to play with our cousins and playmates, Oinam Usharani and Oinam David, we were not permitted beyond the gate. Deep down, we longed to go out and mingle freely with others, and sometimes we couldn't resist doing so. *Ima* understood our desires and occasionally allowed us some freedom, but ensured that we stayed out of trouble and away from bad company.

She had another reason to impose these restrictions: she did not want others calling her children undisciplined or unruly in *Baba*'s absence, as he was often away on duty. Instead of receiving a helping hand, *Ima* often faced judgment and scrutiny for how she raised us. She had to keep a constant vigilance over our activities and whereabouts.

Baba was equally strict, and *Ima* always told us to obey him. One of his strictest rules includes prohibiting us from attending nighttime events such as *Shumang Leela*, an outdoor drama performed by artistes on a raised platform or *Thabal Chongba*, a traditional Meitei moonlight dance where young boys and girls form circles or semi-circles, holding hands and dancing rhythmically to drumbeats under the full moon.

Baba had a valid and grim reason for these restrictions. During those days, many youths were drawn to join insurgency movements in Manipur due to widespread unemployment and limited job opportunities, even for educated youths, in Manipur and other North-eastern states of India. The insurgency conflict was initiated by armed separatist militant groups aiming for secession from India, with members going underground and surfacing to battle with Indian forces. Parents in the region remained vigilant, fearing that their children might be swayed or influenced to join these movements. *Baba*'s strict rules were part of his efforts to protect us from such influences that could lead us astray during those tumultuous times.

The region had seen little development, and there was a widespread perception that the Indian government had not made sincere efforts to address the underlying issues in these states. The law and order situation in our state was unstable, and Manipur had been facing insurgency for a long time.[1] Peace talks and Suspension of Operations (SoO) between the government and the insurgent groups had not yielded lasting results.

Frequent gunfights between the police and insurgent groups were a grim reality. Combing operations conducted by the police and army were very common, often instilling fear in the community. Nighttime operations were particularly dreaded, as all male family members were called out to gather until searches, identifications, and interrogations were over. Whenever we heard a gunshot, which was quite often, we would shout at each other to lie flat on the ground and crawl beneath beds for safety.

However, *Ima* wanted us to know what was happening around us. So she would take us to cultural events like *Shumang Leela* and

---

1 The Manipur kingdom fought a fierce battle against the British army at Khongjom in 1891 during the Anglo-Manipur War but thereafter remained under British colonial rule. The kingdom was later merged with the Indian Union on 15 October 1949. This merger was perceived by many as forced upon Manipur by India, leading to simmering discontent in the state. In the 1960s, the insurgency movement began in Manipur, with various groups emerging determined to achieve what they saw as the "liberation" of Manipur what they viewed as Indian "occupation".

Thabal Chongba when she felt that it was safe for us to venture out. She saw these experiences as opportunities for us to learn about our heritage and understand the social norms of our times.

Ima remained vigilant and attentive to every aspect of our family's needs. She took great care to ensure that we were not led astray or influenced in the wrong direction. While we were not always obedient, the discipline she enforced kept us in good stead. We were by no means the epitome of good behaviour. For instance, when deeply engrossed in play, we often turned a deaf ear to her repeated calls, prompting her to shout at us with all her might to get our attention. Sibling squabbles were a common headache for her, and she did not hesitate to scold us sternly. When we all calmed down, *Ima* would patiently explain the rights and the wrongs of our actions. She would tell us to be careful while playing or interacting with others, and instructed us to avoid unnecessary conflicts.

Ima tried hard to instil in us the values and expectations associated with being part of the Oinam family lineage. She often recounted stories of our grandfather, Oinam Gambhir Singh, who commanded great respect in our locality. After bathing in our pond, he would carry a *chaisel* (a brass utensil used for drinking water) and sprinkle water as he walked, a gesture that ensured no one dared to cross his path. Known for his seriousness, he was a *panji* (a birth chart reader). *Ima* would say that our father had followed in the footsteps of his ancestors, and she encouraged us to uphold the same principles in our conduct. She proudly mentioned our uncles' contributions to the state government—Uncle Oinam Achou in the police department and Uncle Oinam Gokul as the headmaster of a primary school.

For *Ima*, it was not only about instilling the right values in us but also managing the family finances. Instead of relying solely on *Baba* for handling expenses, she preferred to share this responsibility. For her, work was paramount, and she filled her time productively, even during her spare time. In our kitchen garden, she cultivated various vegetables and reared poultry in our small chicken coop. Harvesting vegetables became a family affair, where we all gathered to pluck potatoes, peas, mustard leaves, cabbages, chillis, cucumbers, beans, and tomatoes, filling our *thumok*s with the produce.

As we grew older, *Ima* delegated household chores and responsibilities to each of us. My sisters helped her in the kitchen, taking turns to cook and learn the intricacies of preparing different Manipuri dishes from her. She would tell us that food was an essential part of our lives. We all contributed to the daily tasks: watering the vegetables, feeding the poultry with rice husk powder, chopped cauliflower leaves, and small edible snails. My sisters also assisted *Ima* in weaving and starching nets whenever they could. Meanwhile, my brothers shouldered responsibilities such as taking bags of rice to the mills, ploughing the soil, fetching water from nearby ponds using two *sanaboon*s (traditional water-storing utensils) strapped to bicycles, getting gas cylinders, settling electric bills, cleaning the front and back yards, repairing fences, and collecting woven mosquito nets ordered by *Ima* from local weavers.

Baba and *Ima* were deeply committed to ensuring that we received a quality education that would equip us to succeed in life. They invested a significant portion of their earnings to send us to schools known for their high teaching standards so that they would see their dreams for us fulfilled. Their focus extended beyond conventional academics; they also motivated us to develop practical skills. During vacations, they encouraged us to learn additional courses like typewriting, shorthand, basic computer course, and others. These practical skills bolstered our overall confidence. To further enrich our knowledge and keep us engaged, *Baba* regularly purchased comics, *Reader's Digest*, newspapers, competitive refreshers, and other literature.

We often had tutors to teach us at home. Our first tutor was a lady whom we called *Oja* Tombi from our locality. *Oja* means teacher in the Manipuri language. She was not just a teacher to us but a loyal friend of *Ima*. She used to help *Ima* in little ways, such as carrying us on her back in a baby sling, sometimes baby sitting and also by teaching us. When *Ima* wanted to write letters to *Baba* if he was staying in his police quarters, *Oja* Tombi would help her to do so. She was also an artist and her pencil drawings on pillow covers and handkerchiefs were beautiful. She taught us to draw beautiful scenery and flowers, particularly roses, in very easy steps. She taught us till our mid-classes but then joined a private school in Tamenglong district as a school teacher for four to five years. Even when she stopped teaching us, *Ima* would invite her to dinner and take us to her house.

My older sisters and brothers helped us, the younger lot, in our studies. We all used to study together, sharing the same *kouna* mat, the same candle, *thaomei podhon* or lantern. *Ima* would light up mosquito coils while we studied at night and also used her *inaphee*, swinging it to and fro to ward off mosquitoes. Early in the morning, she would give us tea and snacks and then lay our mats in our front porch for us to study in the sunshine.

Our parents never compared our performance to anybody. We were taught to study hard, but not to outdo anyone. They wanted us to equip ourselves to stand independently, face competitive examinations, and pursue the careers of our choice. Their guiding principle to us was, "You will gain knowledge not just through formal education but also through observation, experience, and your surroundings. Learning is an unending process. Endeavour to behave in such a way that you become a person whom others can look up to, respect, and love."

While we absorbed knowledge from our books, the most important lessons came from observing our parents' hard work, the discipline we learnt from them, the life skills we practised at our home, the mistakes we committed and learnt not to repeat, the punishments we received from our parents that taught us where we were going wrong, and the right advice they gave us in abundance.

6

Demise of *Baba*

Our family life became complete on occasions like *Sajibu Cheiraoba*, Diwali, and *Ningol Chakkouba*. As *Sajibu Cheiraoba* and Diwali approached, we thoroughly cleaned our house a few days in advance, in accordance with the Meitei community traditions. *Ima* would lead us in washing the curtains, removing spider webs, and ensuring every nook and corner of our house sparkled. We would even get down on all fours to sweep under the beds and mop the floor, akin to military trainees crawling under barbed wire! After the cleaning, we decorated our doors and windows with marigold garlands. On Diwali, *Ima* made special garlands to decorate the *chengfu,* followed by prayers, offerings of sweets and fruits to Goddess Lakshmi. After all the rituals were complete, we lit up our front porch with rows of candles. This festival of lights always lifted our spirits.

Sajibu Cheiraoba or *Sajibu Nongma Panba* is the lunar New Year festival of Manipuri people, particularly the Meiteis, whose traditions revolve around Sanamahism, our indigenous religion. It usually falls in April and held significant importance in our family, especially when *Baba* joined us to celebrate. *Baba* and *Ima* always emphasised the importance and traditional practices of *Sajibu Cheiraoba*, teaching us that our thoughts and actions on this day set the tone for the entire year. Therefore, they encouraged us to think positively, avoid arguments, and maintain harmony among ourselves. We had to be kind to each other and maintain peace on this auspicious day.

On *Sajibu Cheiraoba*, *Ima* would rise early to prepare *athenpot* in a big *sengga* (plate), placing rice in the middle surrounded by a variety of vegetables and fruits. This was offered to Lainingthou Sanamahi, the deity from whom our religion derives its name, and Leimarel Ima Sidabi, the mother goddess, with prayers for blessings in the New Year, longevity and good health of all family members, and protection from adversity.

Ima would prepare five or seven curries (it always had to be an odd number), for the offerings, usually a *dal* (lentils) with *uchina* (wood ear mushrooms), *shakthongba* (a mixed vegetable curry), *papad,* and Meitei delicacies like *ooti, eromba, chanakanghou, bora,* and *champhut*. While she prepared the food, *Baba* and my brothers would gather wet mud from our pond and shape it into small, round base outside our gate, marking the area for the prayer offerings. Decorating this base was our task. We collected flowers like *cherei* (*Bougainvillea sp.*), wild roses (*Rosa sp.), jubakusum* or China rose (*Hibiscus sp.*), and April fool flowers *(Amaryllis sp.)* and arranged them artistically around the perimeter of the mud base. The warm April sun quickly dried and solidified the mud base.

Once the preparations were complete, *Ima* would carefully arrange cooked rice in the middle of a clean banana leaf, placing all the curries around it. Betel leaf and areca nuts were presented on a separate rounded banana leaf. *Baba* would then carry these banana leaves to the prayer site for the offerings to the deities of our land, invoking blessings for a prosperous year with his prayer to local deities: "*Lamsenba, Tusemba, Lamapa, Tumapa, Hanu Kokchao, Hanu Leikham*". We all joined him in this prayer.

After the prayer offerings, the highlight of *Sajibu Cheiraoba* awaited us—the communal meal. Gathered together, we savoured the diverse curries lovingly prepared by *Ima.* We ensured there was enough food to share with our neighbours. We then visited their houses to give the prepared curries. In return, our neighbours would also share their own dishes with us, observing a tradition called *ensanglannaba,* symbolising harmonious relations with neighbours.

After this exchange, *Baba* would escort *Ima* to her maternal house, where she presented gifts, primarily clothes, to her brothers and sisters as per tradition.

As a daily routine, *Ima* used to keep *Baba's* rice and curry on a *samuk,* and upon returning from work, he would comfortably enjoy his meal seated on the *chakcha fida* in the kitchen. I remember the joy I felt watching him savour each bite, relaxed after a long day.

When I was in the fifth grade, *Baba* announced that we would be moving to a bigger *pucca* house with corridors and a small front porch. When he showed us the blueprint, we all were excited as we envisioned our new home. Construction began around 1995 and was completed in 2000, just as I was preparing for my tenth-grade examinations. It took five long years to build it due to financial constraints that required *Baba* to take out a home loan.

Finally, the much-awaited day arrived, and we moved into our new home—a typical *pucca* structure with three spacious rooms and a long corridor. The front porch, with its white-painted railings, added an attractive touch to our house. The walls were painted in brick-red and grey, preserving the brick decor. Before shifting, the rooms of our old house, situated at the rear of the plot, were integrated into the new construction, giving the entire house the appearance of a long train with rooms in a row.

After the housewarming, we celebrated *Sajibu Cheiraoba* in 2001 with *Baba*. At that time, since he was posted at the Lilong police station as the officer-in-charge, he stayed there, but came home during holidays. *Baba* had many big dreams for our family and was also waiting for his promotion. But his aspirations got shattered as something unexpected happened.

My sister Promila was in her final year of graduation and came out with flying colours when her results were declared—a commendable first class in English Honours. We celebrated this achievement with a grand meal, joined by our happy and proud *Baba*. Afterwards, he returned to his police quarters. A few days later, he came home again and spent the night with us. He was in a cheerful mood, expressing his affection by taking *Ima* out for lunch on his scooter and purchasing new things for each one of us. The next morning, he left for his quarters.

It was early August when, one restless night, *Ima* and my siblings could not sleep. The next morning, the phone rang with the devastating news that *Baba* had been in an accident. We rushed to the Jawaharlal Nehru Institute of Medical Sciences (JNIMS), where he was admitted. Police personnel informed us that *Baba* had been on his morning patrol duty around Lilong when the police jeep, driven by his subordinate officer on a drizzly morning, skidded on the wet road. *Baba*, who was seated in the front seat, crashed into the front windshield of the jeep. We were told that the glass smashed into his neck, injuring his spinal cord. This tragic accident left him paralyzed from his neck down.

His treatment commenced at JNIMS Hospital, where *Ima*, Kemila, Robert, Dhanabati, and Tiken stayed by his side, while Promila and I remained at home. *Baba* required spoon-feeding as he had lost all sensation and mobility. He was conscious but had to be assisted for everything. It was a harrowing experience for us all. Each day, we consulted the medical team and doctors with the aim of getting the best possible treatment for him.

We fervently hoped for *Baba*'s recovery. *Ima* had always been a strong, composed person, capable to handling any hardship or circumstance. But *Baba's* accident was different—it was the first time we saw her nervous and frightened, her usual composure deserting her. All of us were scared. She followed the doctors' guidance and did everything in her power to ensure our father regained his health.

Despite *Ima*'s devoted care, almost two months passed with little improvement. She made the difficult decision to take *Baba* to Guwahati, Assam, for further treatment. We collected all available savings and borrowed funds for the journey. *Baba* was to be brought back home and then taken to Guwahati.

Baba was a police inspector adorned with three stars on his shoulders. His long-awaited promotion to the rank of Deputy Superintendent of Police (DSP) was just days away—he had even sewn new uniforms for the occasion. But fate struck suddenly with the accident. He had hung his new uniforms on his bed pole before the tragic incident occurred. Upon his return home from the hospital that day, we had forgotten to remove them from the pole, and as soon as *Baba* saw them, tears rolled down his cheeks. We immediately took them away, but we knew his dreams and hopes for his promotion had been shattered.

On 7 October 2001, *Baba* was resting at home after his prolonged hospital stay, and I had the chance to serve him food. In the evening, I fed him rice and water. During the night, the doctor arrived for a routine check-up, but later on, he began experiencing complications at an alarming rate. We all rushed to his bedside, and *Ima* noticed he was struggling to breathe. We all tried to help him, but to no avail.

In a state of panic, around 1 a.m., we urgently called for the doctor. Suddenly, the lights went out and it became very dark. Eventually, the doctor and nurse arrived and examined him. However, by 4 to 4.30 a.m., *Baba*'s breathing had become too laboured, his chest visibly heaving. Finally, with a heavy heart, the doctor uttered, "I'm sorry. We won't be able to save him."

We were all gathered in the room, calling out to him, with *Ima* at his side on the bed. She called to him one last time, but there was no response. It was the early morning of 8 October 2001. We realised that it was over. Shocked and unable to believe it, in those first helpless moments, I could only feel numb.

Then *Ima* broke down, her grief unbearable. It was a nightmare for all of us. It seemed like the end of the world, the end of our happiness.

When *Baba* was cremated that day, the police department honoured him with a gun salute. Prayers and the *shraddha* ceremony were held, attended by many friends and relatives. After this, *Ima* and Robert went to Nabadwip in West Bengal to perform the rituals for his mortal remains.

While our family, like many Meitei families, follows Sanamahism, we also adhere to Vaishnavism, a regional variant of Gaudiya Vaishnavism. Nabadwip is considered a holy place in Hinduism, and it is believed that conducting rituals for mortal remains there brings peace to the departed soul.

The atmosphere in our house became sombre. *Ima* struggled to maintain her composure, her grief and cries echoing through the wee hours of the morning, piercing our hearts. We matured overnight, a harsh lesson that life imparted with such cruelty. We had to console *Ima* and ourselves. A sense of responsibility seeped into our veins, as we understood that we had to continue with our lives and cope with the intense grief. We felt adrift as we embarked on a journey we never anticipated—a journey without our dear *Baba*.

For a long time, despair and emptiness engulfed us. *Ima* had lost her companion of over 30 years, a period when they faced hardships, yet built a home filled with love and dreams for the future. Despite her shattered heart and deep sorrow, *Im*a tried to hold herself together during the day, taking care of us and managing the household. It was during the nights, after we had all retired to bed, that she would break down, her cries reverberating through her room. A sense of emptiness and awareness of a void lingered with us for a long, long time.

I was in the eleventh grade, and Tiken was in the twelfth, so we had to return to our regular classes and examination schedules. Dhanabati was studying for her graduation, while Promila had recently graduated from college and expressed a desire to continue her studies, which *Ima* encouraged. Robert explored employment avenues and eventually began teaching at a private school, with Kemila also deciding to pursue a career in teaching.

Everything felt raw for our family—raw in terms of thoughts, experiences, and planning for the future. The entire responsibility of keeping the family afloat fell solely on *Ima*'s shoulders. She received a monthly family pension, which amounted to about two-third of *Baba*'s former salary. She worried about our future, especially because we were all young and in need of guidance and security.

It was hard for *Ima* to cover all our expenses with the family pension. A portion of it went towards repaying the loan *Baba* had taken for our new house, leaving about Rs 10,000 for household expenses and other necessities. Although we knew that *Ima* felt lonely and scared, she tried hard not to show it to us. She stood strong even though she was deeply affected by *Baba*'s departure and the overwhelming fear she must have felt. We depended on her for everything, especially our emotional and moral support.

Ima worked tirelessly selling woollen shawls in *Ima Keithel* to meet all our needs—daily expenditures, education expenses, fees, books, tuition, conveyance, decent clothes, pocket money, and food. She never made us feel discouraged due to financial constraints or lack of time, endeavouring to bring our circumstances back to normal. The worst nightmare had struck us, but we had to adapt to the huge change in our lives.

Often, society views widows as liabilities and predicts a bleak future for them and their families. *Ima* also faced such discouraging attitudes, but she defiantly stood against them. We were disheartened to see that many of our relatives distanced themselves from us after *Baba*'s demise. It seemed they had either pretended to be well-wishers or feared of being approached for help. *Ima* was too self-reliant to seek assistance from anyone. She faced the daunting new circumstances that arose and refused to burden others.

Although we knew she felt vulnerable and shattered inside, *Ima* did not let herself down. She held her self-respect high so that we could overcome any negativity that came our way. We faced many hardships, but we learnt to fight the challenges boldly, following the example *Ima* set. She strengthened her resolve to face life's harsh reality of mothering us as a widow.

Ima's hard times had set in again.

7

Ima and *Ima Keithel*

Ima's dependence on *Ima Keithel* increased immensely after our father passed away. She resumed going to her market stall partly to escape the memories that haunted her at home and partly to mingle with friends, which helped her cope with the pain. Our entire family's expenses depended on the daily sales at *Ima Keithel*. *Ima* used to travel in a rickshaw through the quieter routes behind Governor Road, seeking solace away from crowds. She remained deeply immersed in her sorrow, and it took a long time for her and us to adjust to *Baba*'s absence.

Ima oscillated between grieving for our father and the weight of responsibility she carried. *Ima Keithel* became her sanctuary, providing her the space she needed to regain her strength and confront what fate had imposed on her and our family.

After purchasing *potpham* at *Ima Keithel*, *Ima* redirected her expertise towards woollen handloom products, mainly shawls and stoles. These included *haophee*s, *leiroomphee*s, *luiphee*s, *nupiphee*s, two-ply *kukiphee*s in various colours, and one-ply *manggamphee*s adorned with *linmayek*s (snake motifs). She also sold *samtu pheematek*s (woollen stoles) with designs like *tindongbi* (depicting a silkworm eating a castor leaf) and flower motifs, along with *leiroom*s, *lengyan*s, and *phanek*s featuring floral designs. She also stocked many one-ply warp and two-ply warp plain shawls. The terms used for the shawls and designs were according to the understanding between the women vendors of *Ima Keithel*.[1]

She arranged these shawls in separate columns and neatly displayed them at her *potpham*. She developed connections with skilled weavers across Imphal valley, including areas like Khurai Chingangbam *leikai*, Khurai Heikrumakhong, Lamlong, Napetpalli, Laipham Khunou, Kairang, Singjamei, Kakwa, and Lourel *leikai*. She also sourced woven shawls from independent local weavers hailing from Khabam, Kontha, Hararou, Yumnam Khunou, Sagoltongba, Wangoi, and Lilong Chajing. *Ima* maintained a large stock of shawls both at her stall and at home. She sold her shawls in bulk to vendors in smaller markets such as Kakching, Nambol, Singjamei, Bishnupur, Thoubal, Heirok, Yairipok, and Moirang, as well as to vendors from hill districts.

Traders from neighbouring states often visited *Ima Keithel* to purchase different shawls and *phanek*s from *Ima* for resale. Transitioning her expertise to woollen shawls was not difficult for *Ima* due to her passion for handloom work. Already skilled in weaving *samtu pheematek*s with diverse designs and patterns, *Ima* quickly mastered the art of identifying different woollen shawls and building a new network with woollen shawl weavers, thereby strengthening her connections with skilled weavers from various weaving traditions.

---

1 The nomenclatures for shawls and designs used at *Ima Keithel* are specific to the women vendors there and do not correspond to the actual names used by various communities in their respective dialects.

In the evening, as *Ima* readied to head home, she packed her shawls into two large cotton bags, which she tightly tied. Every morning upon arriving at *Ima Keithel*, she would offer prayers to Keithel Lairembi, the goddess of the market, seeking blessings for a successful day of sales. She would then untie the cotton bags and begin arranging her woollen *phee*s in her *potpham*. *Ima* followed a tradition where she kept the money from *khullangkha kouba* (the first sale of the day) separately. This practice was believed to bring good luck and enhance sales for the rest of the day.

Ima's *potpham* was situated directly across the stalls selling *kanthas*, traditional quilts given to brides as part of the *awunpot*—a collection of marriage gifts from the bride's maternal family to be taken to her new home. Alongside *kanthas,* the *awunpot* included items like a new mosquito net, a *leiroomphee*, and a *luiphee*. So, whenever customers came to purchase *kantha*s, they often turned their attention to the adjacent row of stalls where *leiroomphees* and *luiphees* were displayed. *Ima* patiently waited for her turn to engage with customers as they carefully selected shawls from her collection.

A *leiroomphee* features a white base adorned with intermittent black vertical strips and a continuous red vertical strip near the white border. There are other varieties, such as *khwang leiroom*s, *khwangsabi leiroom*s, and *kon leiroom*s, depending on the types of looms used in their production. On the other hand, a *luiphee* is a plain white shawl, made either from *langjam* (pure cotton) or *samtu* (wool) with a *lui* (a diagonal weft pattern) design. Whenever a bride-to-be purchased a *leiroomphee* or *luiphee, Ima* handed over the shawls graciously, along with blessings for a happy marriage, prosperous life, and healthy offspring. This act of showering blessings on customers was a cherished tradition among the women vendors of *Ima Keithel*, often leaving the brides-to-be blushing.

Sales were low in the off-season, which spans the summer months, but profits soared during the wedding and winter seasons from November to April. *Ima Keithel* buzzed with activity during *Ningol Chakkouba,* a winter festival. *Ima* eagerly waited for this festival, knowing that traditional shawls would be highly sought after by visitors and tourists at *Ima Keithel.* Shawls and stoles were often gifted during official functions and events to dignitaries and important attendees, resulting in sporadic sales. A significant portion of *Ima*'s clientele included defence and paramilitary personnel stationed in Manipur, whom she communicated with in Hindi, a language she had learnt.

Upon returning from *Ima Keithel*, we would inquire about her day. She often responded, "*khullangkha ama kourak ae uchinnachinna*" (At least I had the first sale of the day). In the off-season, she relied on bulk sales to the women vendors in smaller district markets, although profits from these transactions were meagre, usually ranging from Rs 5 to Rs 10 per shawl sold.

One of the shawls in high demand was the *haophee*s, with spear motifs and black borders. To meet customer preferences for quality, *Ima* provided a range of *haophee*s in various colours including red, navy blue, and green. These shawls featured spear designs and were known by different names such as super *tangkhul*s, *khwang haophees* (woven in a *khwang kon*) and *wakambam houra aruba* (larger and wider shawls). Particularly beautiful was the *pungri haophee* pattern, adorned with distinctive *likli* (bottle) motifs.

For budget-conscious customers, *Ima* showed options like *wakambam houra araiba* (smaller shawls), four-ply yarn *haophee*s, four-ply yarn *tongkap ataiba* with vertical lines, four-ply yarn *tongkap taidaba* without vertical lines, and two-ply yarn *bina maraak taidaba* (small-sized *haophee*s). Men's *haophee*s, known as *houra haophees*, were larger in size. Occasionally, customers would just browse the designs and colours without making a purchase, yet *Ima* remained patient with them. Sometimes, she would go through an entire day without selling a single shawl, eventually folding and packing them up as she closed her stall.

Ima would sometimes return from *Ima Keithel* with just enough money for the next day's rickshaw fare. This was a recurring situation during the off-season, as the demand for warm woollen shawls peaked mainly in winter. Those were tough days, filled with uncertainty about what each day would bring. But one thing was always present—her undying fighting spirit. She tackled each day with determination and hope, never yielding to despair.

Ima was not one to give up or blame the world for her hardships. She felt uneasy about taking even a long nap. Every paisa she earned, every drop of sweat shed, and every sale she made after bargaining with her customers—all of it was spent on us. While her daily sales did not amount to much, her earnings ensured that we never went hungry, not even for a single day.

Ima Keithel

Ima Keithel, also widely known as *Ima* Market, *Nupi Keithel,* or *Khwairamband Bazaar*, holds the distinction of being Asia's largest all-women market entirely managed and run by women, making it a unique entity. The term "*Ima*" translates to mother, while "*Keithel*" is a combination of two Manipuri words, "*kei*" meaning store and "*thel*" meaning display. Together, it signifies a designated place where goods are exhibited for exchange, either through barter or monetary transactions. According to the *Khamnung Engal Leishaba*, a text which deals with the mythical origins of the *Keithel* or market, seven "*lairembis*" (goddesses) introduced "*Lai Keithel Kaba*" to sell various articles. Among them were Chingba Leima, who dealt in rice; Pishum Leima, who handled gold and silver; Chinga Leima in vegetables; Waithou Leima in edible oils; and Waisheng Leima in salt cakes.

In *The Evolutionary Growth of the Khwairamband Keithel*, published by the Manipur Research Society, Imphal (2003), the importance and traditions of this market are documented. Over 500 years old, *Ima Keithel* is distinguished by its unique practice where selling and buying of goods are exclusively conducted by women. Men are prohibited from trading and owning stalls in *Ima Keithel*. The exclusive operation of the market by women or *Imas* within the territory of Manipur can be attributed directly to the *Lallup* system. The term *Lallup* derives its literal meaning of "War Club" from the combination of *Lal* meaning war and *Lup*, which translates to club or organisation. In earlier times, in the absence of a regular standing army, in the country, it was the duty of every able-bodied man to serve as a *lanmee* or soldier. When there was peace, men contributed to the construction of infrastructure such as roads, canals, houses, and bridges. *Lallup* mandated that every male between 17 and 60 years render compulsory state service for 10 days out of 40.

While male family members were engaged in *Lallup* and state services, Manipuri women assumed responsibility for daily domestic and mercantile affairs. They managed their households and took charge of family finances. Meitei women not only cultivated paddy fields, and wove textiles but also made handicrafts alongside household duties. They sold their handloom products, handicrafts, and agricultural goods in what came to be known as *Ima Keithel*.

Since its inception, *Ima Keithel* has been pivotal for the survival and sustenance of Manipuri women and their families. Today, it continues to play a very significant role in the state economy, serving as the epicentre of all commercial and socio-economic activities in the state.

The history of Khwairamband *Bazaar* is intertwined with a myth involving Lainingthou Sanamahi, who took the form of a human being and teased Khwai Nungjengbi Chanu, a vendor of edible goods in the market. The woman's anger drew stares from the people of the Khwai area, and from then onwards, the place became known as Khwairamband.

King Khunjaoba (1652–1666 CE) was a ruler deeply committed to the development of Khwairamband. He oversaw the construction of canals and embankments surrounding the Khwairamband area. In 1660, he also ordered the excavation of a moat around Kangla Fort, located in the fortress city of Kangla, an important political and religious centre where the kingdom of Manipur was established. He built a bund along the Naga river to control water inflow into the Khwairamband area.

However, it was Maharaja Chandrakirti Singh (1834–44 and 1850–1866 CE) who took extensive efforts to develop the actual framework of the *Khwairamband Bazaar*. Besides its commercial activities, the market served as a venue for important proclamations. According to *Cheitharol Kumbaba*, the royal chronicle of the erstwhile Meitei kingdom, Maharaj Chandrakirti Singh established rules for Manipuri women concerning their behaviour, diet, dress, and other aspects, with his proclamations prominently displayed in the bazaar. Charitable activities by the Maharajas of Manipur were also conducted there, such as the distribution of paddy to the poor and needy during times of famine and drought.

Ima Keithel, situated at the heart of Imphal, the capital of Manipur, serves as the largest commercial hub in the state, where trade and marketing are carried out. What distinguishes *Ima Keithel* is its community of women vendors who play a central role in this vibrant marketplace. Around 4,000 women operate as registered vendors at *Ima Keithel* under licences issued by the Imphal Municipal Corporation, alongside a sizeable number of 3,000 unregistered street vendors. These women, coming from diverse backgrounds, face significant financial challenges at home.

For many of these women, owning a *potpham* (stall) at *Ima Keithel* is not just a means of livelihood but a dream—a personal workspace where they can independently conduct their business affairs. Here, they manage every aspect of their trade—from transactions and financial calculations to negotiations with *mahajan*s and traders. Every vendor has her own weaving, trading, and marketing strategies.

The majority of women who come to *Ima Keithel* face financial crises at home, which drives them to muster the courage to earn their livelihood. For them, life is not a bed of roses. They have left the comfort of their homes to earn by selling various products such as vegetables, handloom items, handicrafts, pottery, fish, flowers, candles, pickles, incense sticks, and any other goods that can generate income. Ultimately, *Ima Keithel* gives them an opportunity to strengthen their finances and acts as a platform for enhancing their social and political awareness, alongside economic empowerment. It also contributes to boosting the local economy.

Ima belonged to this hard-working community. *Ima Keithel* springs to life in the wee hours of the morning when women from the hills and valleys arrive with their locally grown organic products. These include fresh fruits, vegetables, fish, homemade snacks, salt cakes, traditional handlooms, handicrafts, and other local goods. Registered vendors occupy their *potpham*s within the market, while street vendors line the roadside. They remain there until their goods are sold for the day, enduring the scorching heat, cold, or rain, and confronting the unpredictable daily weather conditions. Very often, they are chased by patrolling policemen tasked with clearing the market's pathways and traffic. These vendors then run away with their bamboo baskets balanced on their heads, seeking another suitable spot to sell their products. They may settle on the steps of the three markets, in the passageways between the *Keithels,* or in any available corner they can find.

Ima Keithel, with its huge expanse of more than 5,000 stalls and spread across three buildings, is stacked with everything one can possibly think of—from betel leaves and areca nuts to religious products like incense sticks, fine *kouna* mats, blankets, and various food items. It stands as a testimony to the entrepreneurship, passion, and determination displayed by its women vendors.

Moreover, *Ima Keithel* serves as a crucial lifeline for many weavers from urban, rural, and hill areas who sell their handloom products to the women vendors. The vendors procure these handcrafted products in bulk and later sell them to customers. In rural Manipur, nearly every household owns a loom. Manipuri handlooms such as Rani *phees* made from pure mulberry silk, Khurkhul *muga* suits (*muga* being silk from the cocoon of a moth; Khurkhul is a village in Imphal West), and cotton traditional drapes like Moirang *phee* and Wangkhei *phee* are known for their fine quality and beautiful designs.

Traditional shawls and garments, alongside a diverse array of local handicrafts and handlooms, are sold in *Ima Keithel.* It has become a focal point for over 2 lakh handloom weavers in Manipur, with women comprising 99 per cent of this workforce. According to the 4th National Handloom Census Reports (2019-20), there are about 2,21,855 handloom worker household in Manipur of which 1,92,431 are in rural weaver households and 29,424 in urban settings.

Ima and other women vendors in the three *Ima Keithel*s procure handloom products from weavers who travel from various parts of the state to sell at *Ima Keithel.* These vendors also establish networks with weavers across different localities. The weavers empower themselves economically, achieving financial independence through their looms. Weaving is a primary occupation for women in both rural and urban areas of the valley region of Manipur.

In the same way, women living in the hills either work on their looms and make bamboo products or are occupied in farming activities such as tending to cattle and poultry, collecting water for irrigation, and ploughing the land. These economic pursuits not only enhance their family finances but also provide opportunities for self-employment.

The contribution of Manipuri women to society is tremendous. Known for their industrious and entrepreneurial spirit, the majority of rural Manipuri women are involved in weaving, fishing, farming, crafting handmade goods, salt production (making salt cakes from salt well water), and various small-scale production activities such as food processing, incense stick and candle making, as well as bamboo and cane crafts. Doll making, particularly the creation of traditional *laiphadibi*s (cloth dolls), is a distinctive craft of the valley. These dolls are crafted from raw materials like fabric, clay or corn husk, sometimes stuffed, and decorated suitably. Besides being playthings, they are revered as spirits that guide and protect Manipuris.

Kouna craft is another popular indigenous craft practised by Manipuri women, which gives them substantial earnings. The raw material used is water reed plants, commonly known as *kouna*, which grow naturally in shallow lakes, marshy lands, canals, and wetlands. A diverse range of eco-friendly handicraft products made from *kouna* includes bags, baskets, containers, mats, hats, boxes, cushions, and mattresses.

The valley region of Manipur is known for its traditional methods of moulding pots and earthen toys, while the famous Longpi pottery is made in Ukhrul, the hill district of Manipur. Fashioned from brown clay found only in Ukhrul's Longpi village, this pottery is unique because it does not involve the use of a pottery wheel. Another distinctive product is found in the Andro area of Imphal East district, where coil pottery items used as utensils for cooking are exclusively made by married women.

A variety of earthen pots such as pitchers, flower vases, pots, lamps, incense stands, toys, and figurines are created by women who bring their handlooms, vegetable produce, or finished handicraft products to sell at *Ima Keithel*. The market provides a platform primarily for widows, elderly women, both married and unmarried women to engage in economic activities within a free and safe environment. Trading independently allows them decision-making autonomy, particularly in how they choose to spend their earned income, which usually covers healthcare, education for their children, and other family expenses.

In her book, *My Three Years in Manipur*, Ethel St. Clair Grimwood, whose husband was the British political agent in Manipur in the early 1890s, noted:

> The women did all the hard work, as a rule. They wove all their own and their husbands' clothing, and cooked and looked after the house generally, besides working in the fields and coming every evening to the big bazaar with merchandise for

> sale or exchange. No men were allowed to sell in this bazaar with the exception of a few Bengalee traders, who sat in a different part of the market and sold cloths. It was a pretty sight in the evening to see all the women hurrying along with their wares on their heads, and their little babies slung on their backs. They sat in long rows in the bazaar, and it was divided up in a most methodical way. Vegetables and fish occupied one end, and cloths and jewellery the other, and the whole of the female population turned out, and even the princesses occasionally sold in the bazaar.

Also, the noted scholar and writer on Indian tribes, T.C. Hodson, in his book *The Meitheis* wrote his observation on Manipuri women, "The women hold a high and free position in Manipur, all the internal trade and exchange of the produce of the country being managed by them."

Truly, Manipuri women are hardworking and courageous, who oversee their day-to-day domestic and mercantile affairs and shoulder major responsibilities in running their families alongside their menfolk. *Ima Keithel* plays a significant role in empowering Manipuri women in their daily struggle for survival.

Structure of Ima Keithel

E.W. Dun, in the *Gazetteer of Manipur* (1885; Delhi reprint, 1975, p. 64) writes, "There is no attempt in any of the market places as the erection of shelter of any kind, and the women remain exposed to rain or sun ...". In short, marketplaces in Manipur did not have any urban facilities during the pre-British period. After the British occupied Kangla Fort on 27 April 1891, *Khwairamband Bazaar* remained closed for one month. The British began preparations to construct a women's market as early as 1892, erecting some huts with thatched roofs. Unfortunately, these were prone to fires due to the inflammable material used for thatching. To address this, the sheds were roofed with corrugated iron sheets in 1905. Such governmental measures were appreciated by the women working in the market. Although there was an office called Keithel Awomba Loishang to manage the bazaar affairs during the pre-British period, the municipal administration of Imphal was established only recently.

Let me share an account by Jarnail Singh, IAS (Retd) on the measures taken to improve the *Ima* Markets in Imphal during his tenure as the Project Director of the Manipur Development Society and Commissioner of the Public Works Department (PWD) under the Manipur government. In 1994, when Manipur was under President's rule, Lieutenant General V.K. Nayar (Retd) was the Governor and took a keen interest in developing the infrastructure of the three *Ima* Markets in the heart of the Imphal city. Despite being centres of economic activity, these markets had seemingly not seen repairs since their original construction three or four decades ago. Governor Nayar personally visited the *Ima* Markets accompanied by his Advisor, P.P. Srivastava, IAS (Retd) and Jarnail Singh. The floors of the marketing sheds were mostly *kacha,* made of clay, with only a few supported by bricks. The plinths were low, and the drains around the sheds were non-functional, causing water to collect and stagnate during rains, particularly on the western side, creating breeding grounds for mosquitoes and insects. During floods, water would inundate these markets, forming stagnant pools. This situation occurred regularly due to the narrowing of the Nambul River behind Paona Bazaar, caused by encroachments, road construction, and the old Jiribam bus stand on river's western side.

The roofs of the *Ima* Markets urgently needed repairs as many were leaking. In spite of the neglected condition of the marketing sheds, the *Ima*s would start their business early in the morning and continue selling their products till late evening. After dark, these vendors would light kerosene lamps to carry on with their sales. The government held discussions with the *Ima*s to propose improvements for the *Ima* Markets. The proposal included raising the plinths by about three feet and making them *pucca*, replacing the roofing with corrugated galvanised iron (GCI) sheets, installing electrical points at all locations in the marketing sheds, providing hooks for vendors to hang their clothes, and renovating the drains.

Although the entire cost of the repair work was to be borne by the government, the *Ima*s initially did not agree to the proposal. Since 1972, successive state governments had attempted to improve the *Ima* Markets, but vendors had consistently resisted. On further interactions with the vendors, Jarnail Singh learnt that they harboured fears that their current spaces would be taken away after repairs. They believed the state government might allocate their spaces to others, often relatives of ministers, MLAs, and officers. This concern had not been satisfactorily addressed, leading to delays in market repairs, despite plans by the Department of Municipal Administration, Housing, and Urban Development (MAHUD) to construct a new market in Lamphel.

After several meetings and assurances from the state government, vendors agreed to allow repairs to commence. They were promised that all *Imas* would be videotaped in their current spaces, and each space would be numbered. This was intended to ensure that, after repairs, all women vendors would return to their original spaces in the sheds. With the vendors' confidence secured, repair work began. Temporary spaces were given for two months during construction so vendors could continue selling their products.

The Public Works Department (PWD) and the Manipur Development Society (MDS) jointly initiated the repair work. Jarnail Singh monitored progress at the construction site almost daily. The construction was to be completed within 60 days, with engineers from PWD and MDS working diligently. A challenging task was bending the GCI sheets into semi-circular shapes to replace the roofs of the market sheds.

As promised, the improved market was completed within the stipulated 60 days. The state government handed over all the seating spaces to the *Ima*s, who resumed their transactions from their original, now repaired and renewed spaces.

In 2005, the old *Ima* Markets were demolished and replaced with new structures. During the reconstruction into the present-day *Ima Keithel*s, all women vendors united to voice their concerns to state authorities. They spent sleepless nights in their *potpham*s as a mark of protest against the reconstruction. *Ima* also joined the protest, enduring the cold winter season. Their determined stance continued for weeks until state government assured them that all their concerns would be taken into account. This demonstrated their unwavering commitment to defending their rights.

Construction finally began later that year. The government erected a temporary market shed to accommodate all vendors from the three *Ima Keithel*s. It was congested and suffocating; tin roofs became burning hot in summer, making conditions unbearable. Nonetheless, *Ima* and other vendors had to bear the heat daily. Construction continued for almost five years.

The newly constructed *Ima Keithel* was inaugurated in 2010. It was given a traditional architectural design featuring tiered and pointed rooftops. *Ima* got her *potpham,* as did all other registered vendors after verifying their vendor cards.

Ima Keithel is a conglomerate of three market buildings: Leimarel Sidabi *Ima Keithel,* Phouoibee *Ima Keithel* adjacent to Thangal Bazaar, and Emoinu *Ima Keithel* (or Laxmi *Ima Keithel*) adjacent to Paona Bazaar. *Ima's* stall was at Laxmi *Ima Keithel.* In the renovated *Ima Keithel,* Laxmi *Keithel* stands somewhat isolated from the other two, attracting fewer visitors than the northern-side *Keithel*s. All the three markets have upper floors that were rarely used until recently, when new stalls were also constructed on the first floor. The *potpham*s are open stalls arranged in rows and sections, with several blocks running parallel to each other. About four vendors comfortably fit in each section of a row, each *potpham* standing on a raised platform.

Following the footsteps of earlier vendors, present-day women vendors sell a diverse array of items. These include exquisite handlooms, traditional costumes and handicrafts, shawls, sarongs, mufflers, jewellery, wicker works, basketry, mosquito nets, utensils, flowers, knives, betel leaves, areca nuts, household tools, mud pots, fruits, vegetables, *soibum* (fermented bamboo shoots), *thum mapak* (salt plates), freshly caught fish, *ngari* (fermented fish), and many other local and non-local products.

Every row in the market shed specialises in specific items, maintaining uniformity throughout. For example, rows dedicated to traditional dresses like *mayeknaibi phanek,* both cotton and acrylic, adorned with the Moirang *pheejin* design at the border are clustered together. Another row offers only silk *phanek* suits with matching drapes, silk sarees, silk *pheematek*s, and silk shirting materials, particularly for *pumyat*s (upper dress for males). There are also rows selling *khudei*s and *pheijom*s (male attire) alongside ordinary cotton *phaneks*. Rows showcasing Rani *phees* made of mulberry silk yarn with Moiranthem *mayeks* and intricate extra weft designs, and Wangkhei *phees* embellished with colourful flower motifs and Moirang *pheejin* on the borders are also present. There are rows selling shirts and clothes for children and women, as well as rows dedicated to woven towels, pillow covers, handloom bedsheets, both in acrylic and cotton with flower designs and different patterns.

Ima's row specialises in traditional woollen shawls, including those made with acrylic wefts, featuring tribal motifs, among other diverse shawls. Adjacent vendors exclusively sell *kanthas* and pillows, while another row behind *Ima* offers a variety of *phaneks*. Further rows specialise in selling mosquito nets, puffed rice, sweet puffed rice balls, and ritual items for both Sanamahism and Hinduism, such as deity clothes, dyed flags, *chandan* (sandalwood), *charik*, small mirrors, and pure cotton threads. Separate rows cater to household items like locally made knives in various sizes and designs, as well as brass utensils and items. Essentially, any item under the sun can be found in *Ima Keithel*.

Ima was accompanied by her fellow vendors, namely, Laishram Mema, Laishram Manorama, Bala, Anita alias Leima, Robini, Keinahanbi, Binasakhi, Nalini, Lourembam Mema, Thoibi, Bilashini, Bamon Mema, and Ebenungshi. When addressing older vendors, she respectfully added *Iche* to their names, such as *Iche* Mema and *Iche* Ebenungshi, while younger vendors called her *Ima Memcha*. Over time, *Ima* became a veteran vendor. She had struggled to establish her presence among the women vendors. Initially, when she purchased her *potpham* and started selling her shawls, many veteran vendors interfered in her sales by diverting interested customers away from her stall. However, as they observed how she held her ground, they eventually gave up their inconsiderate and unprofessional behaviour.

Ima treated younger vendors with kindness and respect, allowing them the opportunity to make their own sales.

Ima earned the love and respect of her fellow vendors through her behaviour. She had a dear friend from Tera, a locality in Imphal West, whom she affectionately called *Iche* Thambalngou. She sold *kantha*s and *leiroomphee*s in a different row, two rows ahead of *Ima*'s stall. Since she did not have many items to sell, she often came to *Ima* to borrow *leiroomphee*s and *luiphee*s, which *Ima* generously shared with her. *Ima* also ensured that they shared the profits from these sales. She frequently gave shawls to her friend for her *potpham*. Other vendors envied their camaraderie, but no one dared to interfere in their close friendship. Aunt Thambalngou, being much older than *Ima,* wholeheartedly supported her and used her dominating voice to ensure no one obstructed their bond.

Ima's fellow vendors were competitive during auspicious days when customers thronged *Ima Keithel,* but during off-season, they gathered to share tea, snacks and gossip, laughing away their worries. Most of them bonded strongly with each other.

Ima never forgot her responsibilities and often bought items like brass and steel utensils, which she considered essential for her four daughters' future weddings. She carefully wrapped these items in paper and polythene, preparing them for inclusion in their trousseaus, as per tradition in the Meitei community. When asked why she bought these things ahead of time, she explained, "I am buying these items now because I know it won't be possible for me to buy everything at once when each of your weddings comes. I want to be prepared so that there is no panic at that point."

She made these purchases whenever she had good profits and on auspicious days like *Kwak Jatra* (Dussehra). With foresight, she also stocked up groceries such as pulses, salt, sugar, and rice in large quantities whenever her profits allowed. This preparation helped her manage during lean periods or when *Ima Keithel* remained closed due to *bandh*s and blockades on the National Highways, which were common tactics to press demands on the state government. These disruptions caused severe economic hardships as they could last for months, and particularly affected the common people the most, preventing them from conducting their transactions or running their businesses.

Ima Keithel was an abode for *Ima* and for us, almost akin to a place of worship. She deeply believed in Goddess Keithel Lairembi and regularly offered prayers to Keithel Lairembi and Lairemba, the female and male deities of *Ima Keithel*, seeking their blessings. *Ima* often told us, "Everything I have been able to accomplish—my sales, profits, and ability to provide for our family—is blessed by Keithel Lairembi. Never take Keithel Lairembi lightly and always have faith in Her."

Ima definitely had a distinctive aura that drew people to her. Many customers who bought her woollen shawls often mentioned that they bypassed other vendors as soon as they saw *Ima,* feeling an immediate inclination to buy from her. She consistently ensured her customers' satisfaction with fair and honest deals. Beyond maintaining warm relations and business connections with traders, customers, and weavers from different regions, she also forged strong bonds with her fellow vendors. For *Ima*, *Ima Keithel* was not just a workplace; it was a space she had earned—a place that gave her a livelihood and a close circle of friends.

Ima Keithel had also become a gathering point for our family. Sometimes, by chance, or due to our desire to see *Ima*, we would visit her there. Her friends would tease me when I arrived at her stall, saying, "Here comes the last one! Your sisters have already been and gone, and now it's your turn."

Ima would always smile warmly and make space for me to sit beside her. Amidst the bustling noise of the market, we would sip tea together, and I always felt a sense of peace in her company. Everything about *Ima Keithel*—*Ima*'s *potpham*, her friends, the diverse aromas, and racket in *Ima Keithel*—had become integral parts of our lives, creating a place where we felt comfortable and happy. Her friends would share their snacks with us, and together, we enjoyed the best lunchbreaks. Sometimes, we would venture to the first floor of Laxmi *Keithel*, where a fast-food restaurant offered rice, *paratha*, *pakoras*, and other snacks. There, we would order what we wanted to eat, chat, and relax for a while.

Ima shared light-hearted moments as well as her joys and sorrows with her fellow vendors, who had become her extended family. She had carved out her own identity through sheer hard work. She had started her journey in *Ima Keithel* as a means to support our family financially, and she initially went through the tough phase of relying on her daily sales, which sometimes barely covered our expenses. Over time, visiting *Ima Keithel* became her daily routine, where she not only conducted business but also found cheerful moments with her friends. She had friendly relations not only with vendors in Laxmi *Keithel* but also with those in the other two *awang* (northern) *Ima Keithel*s.

Ima Keithel has flourished since time immemorial and will continue to do so, providing a haven for the resilient entrepreneurs of Manipur and empowering them to overcome challenges. For *Ima,* her connection with *Ima Keithel* gave her the strength to shoulder huge responsibilities she carried and to face them with fortitude.

8

The Lone Journey

Ima was articulate, yet not outspoken. Even when she must have had unfulfilled desires, she rarely spoke about them. Whenever our rights felt threatened, such as issues with land demarcation or other matters, she let Baba decide what to do and how to deal with the issue or the person who brought it up, be it family members or neighbours. However, after *Baba* passed away, many changes unfolded. *Ima* began asserting her authority and took sole responsibility, even if it required speaking out strongly on our behalf. She remained like a mountain for us to rely upon, confident that she would safeguard us. As our own challenges began emerging, each of us contemplated our future careers and the paths we would take. *Ima* had unwavering faith in us, knowing that with persistent effort and dedication, we would find our paths. She never pressured us at any point, even if we failed in our various attempts in examinations or in the work we chose to do. Instead, she instilled the courage we needed to face failure and hardships.

One gift *Ima* gave us through her example was hope, for she never gave up. Although she experienced despair after losing *Baba*, each day saw her gradually but surely replace it with her dedication to work, her concern for our studies, the needs of our family, and our future. Her hopes for us motivated us to work harder to become dedicated to our chosen paths.

As time passed, *Ima* and all of us were back on track and had adapted to the void left by *Baba*'s absence. Kemila and Robert had been teaching in private schools for a few years, and soon it was time for their marriages. Organising a wedding involves meticulous planning, managing expenses, and ensuring all traditional customs are observed—a significant undertaking in any society, particularly in Meitei culture where weddings are grand and financially demanding. Since we were in the lower-middle-income group, arranging these weddings posed a major challenge for *Ima*. She tackled this responsibility with careful planning, drawing on her savings and the contributions of my older siblings, who also pitched in with their savings.

Baba had passed away when he was only in his early 50s and all of us were still very young. When our weddings took place, *Ima* managed the ceremonies with utmost care and attention to detail. Her foresight and preparation ensured everything went smoothly, and we were blessed by her for our new lives ahead.

In Manipuri society, the term "marriage" is known as *luhongba*. The first *luhongba* ceremony in our family was for my eldest brother, Robert (whom I called *Dada*). When *Dada* married Saikhom Anita from Soibam *Leikai*, Imphal East district, it marked a joyous occasion for our family after a long time.

In Meitei tradition, the marriage ceremony is preceded by the *heijing-kharai puba* (engagement), also known as *heijingpot*, followed by the *mapam chakkouba*—a grand luncheon at the bride's home to welcome the newly-wed couple, held five days after the marriage. As my brother's wedding approached, minor renovations and whitewashing of our house were done. Invitations were distributed to all our relatives, friends, and neighbours, detailing the dates of these three ceremonies: *luhongba, heijingpot*, and *mapam chakkouba*.

To prepare for the ceremonies, a temporary tin roof was erected over our entire front verandah supported by bamboo poles. Skilled persons were hired to set up the *shamiyana* (tent), lighting, and decorations for the wedding. Brahmins and *arangphams*—professionals skilled in organising wedding rituals—were also arranged. *Ima* procured all necessary items and ordered mandatory puffed rice packets and various food items for the *heijingpot* and wedding day.

For the *heijingpot* ceremony, *Ima* invited married ladies from our locality to carry the *phiruk* and *heijingkharai*—ceremonial baskets filled with fruits, rice, betel leaves, areca nuts, and other items signifying good wishes for couple's welfare, prosperity, and long life. The *heijingpot* involved the exchange of items between elders of the bride's and groom's families, followed by offerings and prayers to Sanamahi and other deities. Fruits, puffed rice, and packed food items were distributed to all attendees.

At the conclusion of the *heijingpot*, the bride's mother handed over the *kundali* (horoscope) of the bride to *Ima*, after which they exchanged betel leaves with areca nuts. Traditional dresses for my sister-in-law were given to her family.

The day before the *luhongba* ceremony, which was to be held at the bride's residence, a young boy from her family accompanied by an elder male relative visited us to formally invite *Dada*—a practice known as *bor baton touba* in Meitei tradition.

On the day of the wedding, *Dada* wore a *pungyat* (upper body dress), *pheijom* (dhoti), and a *kokyet* (headdress), all in white. The wedding procession began from our residence with a ritual known as *borjatra*, where prayers were offered for an auspicious wedding and blessings were sought from the groom's mother and elder relatives to start the procession. The wedding ceremony took place at the bride's home, attended by our family members and relatives.

We eagerly awaited the return of the wedding procession and the arrival of the bride at our home. As soon as they entered with other guests, everyone rushed to catch a glimpse of the bride. *Ima* warmly embraced my sister-in-law and ushered her into her new home. Together, we proceeded to the room where we worshipped Lainingthou Sanamahi and Leimarel Sidabi to seek blessings, and then escorted her to her new room. Soon after, guests streamed in, filling our house, and we were all on our toes serving food and tea to all. The wedding day wrapped up with a grand family dinner.

The weddings of my sisters were altogether different affairs. Kemila's (whom I called *Cheche*) wedding provided a better understanding into the preparations undertaken by a bride's family. *Ima* meticulously arranged the *awunpot*, comprising essential gifts for the trousseau such as traditional brass utensils, a *luiphee*, a *leiroom phee*, *kantha*s, and additional items like furniture and gold ornaments. The wedding *mandap* was erected in our front verandah.

Ima selected a talented *Nupa Pala*, who sang Manipuri *Nat Sankirtana* songs and performed the *pung chollom*—a traditional Meitei dance performed to the rhythmic beat of *pung*s (drums). She also enlisted the guidance of a seasoned *keinasennabi* to assist the bride throughout the ceremony.

A Meitei bride's attire includes a *phanek*, adorned with either a *kajeng lei* (for those who follow only Sanamahism) or a *potloi*—a stiff cylindrical skirt in red or green, intricately decorated with traditional motifs, small mirrors and other embellishments (for those who follow Vaishnavism). On her wedding day, *Cheche* looked resplendent in a *potloi* paired with a velvet blouse, a rich fabric in green, covered by a starched white drape edged with golden borders. *Ima,* radiating elegance, wore a starched white Wangkhei *phee* embellished with beautiful *lamthangkhullak mayek* (motifs) and a *thamballeikhok mapannaibi phanek*. Other elder women were also dressed in white Rani *phee*s or starched Wangkhei *phee*s with various floral motifs. This ensemble created a uniform and elegant look, further enhanced by the addition of pink *mapannaibi phanek*s. The rest of us, including unmarried girls, donned colourful *Rani phees* with matching *mapannaibi phanek*s.

The Manipuri *Sankirtana* singing commenced before the groom's party arrived, performed with grace by the *Nupa Pala,* while the rhythmic *pung chollom* music reverberated in the wedding *mandap*. Guests were seated on long *kouna* mats, arranged in rows around the *mandap*.

A major ritual in the wedding is the *kujaba punba*, symbolising the union of the bride and groom as they begin their new life together. During this ritual, *Ima* tied *Cheche*'s hands with my brother-in-law's using a sacred thread. Men and women of all ages formed a line to individually give good wishes and blessings to *Cheche* and her groom after the *kujaba punba*. *Cheche* then circled her groom, who remained seated on the *luhong phan* (groom's seat), seven times, and the marriage ceremony ended with them garlanding each other with *kundo pareng* (a flower from the jasmine family, which symbolises witness to the wedding). *Cheche*'s husband, Bobby Loitongbam, hails from Imphal West district. Amidst the joyousness and gaiety, we bade her farewell.

Ima remained at our home while the bridal procession headed to the groom's residence. The *mapam chakkouba* was hosted at our residence five days after the wedding, where both our family members and *Cheche*'s in-laws gathered to interact and feast.

These marriage ceremonies held significant importance for *Ima* as she considered them her major responsibility. They also meant the beginning of a new journey for us with our life partners. During these momentous occasions, *Ima* always remembered *Baba* and would tell us wistfully, "I wish *Baba* was here with us to share these joyful moments and bless you all. I'm sure he is watching us all from above."

I had begun attending Ghanapriya Women's College, following in the footsteps of Promila and Dhanabati. Promila had already completed her graduation and was pursuing further studies at Manipur University. After her graduation, Dhanabati initially enrolled in a hotel management course sponsored by the Tourism Department of the Government of Manipur but later switched to teaching at a private school. *Damcha* was studying at the Dhanamanjuri College of Science, the same institution *Cheche* had attended, while *Dada* had graduated from the Dhanamanjuri College of Arts.

We went to our colleges or the university by public transport, which was mainly buses or canters (small light-duty vehicles). *Damcha* did not mind going to college on his bicycle and rarely complained about it. He would only use *Baba*'s Bajaj scooter on special occasions. We were mindful of our expenses to lessen the financial burden on *Ima*. I enjoyed cycling to my National Cadet Corps (NCC) classes and activities on Sundays at the Dhanamanjuri College campus during my college days.

We were all exploring various career paths. Since competitive examinations were the primary route to success, *Ima* time and again reminded us to focus on our studies and take responsibility for our own futures.

Damcha aimed to join the Indian Army, while I was fascinated by the Indian Air Force and aspired to become a pilot in its flying branch. Both of us successfully completed the course to earn "C" certificates in the NCC under No.1 Air Squadron (Flg), Senior Air Wing NCC Unit, Imphal as senior air wing cadets during our college days. *Ima* encouraged us to not only participate in NCC activities locally but also in camps outside the state. She believed in the importance of exploring the world and gaining diverse experiences. The NCC taught us about many things, but primarily we learnt about national integration during the camps where we interacted with cadets from various states of India. These interactions exposed us to different cultural aspects such as songs, dances, dresses, and languages.

Ima never missed watching us participate in Republic Day parades in Imphal. Her presence in the crowd, gathered to witness contingents in smart uniforms marching in the parades, filled us with delight and pride. When Republic Days and Independence Days were boycotted by underground organisations and the state observed complete shutdowns, *Ima* and Dhanabati would walk from our house up to Keishampat and Kangla just to see us, which greatly boosted our morale.

In every stage of her life, *Ima* always listened to her inner voice, unafraid to voice her opinions when she knew she was right. While her decisions influenced our lives in many ways, she always gave us the freedom to listen to our conscience. From selecting our courses of study, careers, friends, and life partners to participating in extracurricular activities and preparing for competitive exams, we siblings exercised our own decision-making from an early age. She placed her trust in us and encouraged us to appear for various competitive exams, whether for state or central jobs. *Ima* constantly urged us to keep moving and never give up until we succeeded in our endeavours. She would patiently discuss important matters with us, listening attentively before offering insights.

During our college days, *Ima* used to wake us around 4.30 a.m. for our morning walk, even before dawn broke. *Damcha* jogged while Dhanabati and I opted for brisk walking alongside *Ima*. She walked so fast that sometimes we had to run to keep up with her. Our route was about 4 kilometres from our home to Little Flower School or sometimes up to the Iskcon temple, where we would turn back. She was strong and healthy—passers-by and fellow walkers often remarked on her fitness. The cool morning breeze gave us a fresh start for the day and the walk energised us. For *Ima,* these morning walks were essential for maintaining her health and gave her the strength to accomplish her daily tasks.

However, challenges continued to arise in our family. One evening after dinner, *Damcha* suddenly developed severe abdominal pain and had to be rushed to the Regional Institute of Medical Sciences (RIMS), Imphal. The doctor diagnosed him with appendicitis requiring immediate surgery. He was in his second year of graduation. It happened so suddenly. *Ima* did not delay and followed the doctor's advice very carefully. Much to our relief, the operation was successful. For her, nothing was more important than the safety of her children. Initially concerned about *Damcha*'s career prospects in the armed forces due to the surgery, we were reassured that minor operations like appendectomy did not hinder enlistment. *Ima* felt immense relief knowing that *Damcha* would recover and could continue pursuing his dream.

Ima's struggle to meet our everyday expenses continued. Since the income from selling shawls at *Ima Keithel* was insufficient, she took mini-loans from moneylenders who collected repayments daily at a minimal interest rate from her at *Ima Keithel.* She explored various avenues to supplement our income, including selling charcoal during winter seasons. Every morning and evening, before and after her days at *Ima Keithel*, she would sell charcoal packets stocked at our *pakhan* (a small lodging) in front of our house. She packed them in small packets, priced at Rs 20 each, which were popular among people in our neighbourhood. Although we tried to assist whenever possible, *Ima* insisted we focus on our studies. Every bit of profit made was important and valuable to her.

Despite her tireless efforts, bad misfortune occasionally threw obstacles in her path. One day, while filling charcoal packets, *Ima* slipped and hurt her wrist. The doctor diagnosed a dislocated bone. So she had to go through a painful procedure to reset it. Advised to rest until her recovery, she felt restless and helpless staying idle for the two to three months it took for her hand to heal fully. We urged her to rest and stop worrying, although setbacks like this allowed herself some much-needed rest.

Before his marriage, Robert completed his graduation with history as his major and later pursued a Bachelor's in Education (BEd) as an additional course. He opened a hardware store in Uripok after marriage, leaving his teaching job at a private school due to inadequate salary. After the birth of his first child, Angelina, in 2007, Robert secured a position as an arts graduate teacher under the Education Department of the government of Manipur. This achievement was a dream come true for all of us, especially *Ima,* who had seen the prevalent corruption in the process of obtaining such positions through bribes or influence. *Dada*'s success became a beacon of hope and happiness in our lives, restoring our faith in the government and bringing immense joy to *Ima.*

Ima continued to be a guiding light for us, especially inspiring us to pursue competitive examinations. Kemila had left her teaching job after marriage and faced the challenges of early motherhood while raising two sons. Following our mother's advice, she took many competitive examinations and eventually got selected as a Sarva Shiksa Abhiyan (SSA) primary teacher under the state government.

Promila married R.K. Parashmani, her classmate from Manipur University, and despite the added responsibilities, she earned her Master's and doctoral degree (PhD). Nevertheless, she kept her aspiration to become a lecturer burning for years. In 2018, her dedication and hard work paid off when she was selected as an assistant professor in the Education Department. Dhanabati initially taught in a private school and later joined the Manipur Police as a constable. She married Soram Rincoo from Imphal West.

My sisters drew inspiration from *Ima*, who served as a role model during their journey into motherhood. She gave them practical advice and health tips to strengthen them mentally and physically. During the early months after each delivery, *Ima* would stay at her daughter's home to help her with the newborn baby and take care of her health, all the while managing her business at *Ima Keithel.* The marriages of my siblings and the births of niece and nephews brought immense joy and hope into our lives. *Ima*'s first grandchild, Angelina Oinam, was adored dearly by her. She would cradle Angelina lovingly in her arms, gently rocking her to sleep in a baby sling on her back. Her affection for all her grandchildren was evident and heartfelt.

As soon as he completed his graduation, *Damcha* sat for the Combined Defence Services (CDS) examination and got selected for a Short Service Commission in the Indian army. He opted to join the army and did not pursue further studies. In my final year of graduation, I also took the Air Force Common Admission Test conducted by the IAF in Varanasi. Despite *Ima*'s reservations about my joining the active forces, she encouraged me to pursue my dream and go to Varanasi for the exams. *Damcha* and I boarded the train from Guwahati to Mughalsarai and then reached Varanasi by road. We stayed in a hotel near the examination centre.

At the examination venue, I met my NCC friend Aradhana from Lucknow. We were briefed on the three-tier examination process, comprising a written test, a Pilot Aptitude Battery Test (PABT), and a viva voice. After successfully passing the written test, I advanced to the PABT, a once-in-a-lifetime test. I was given a headphone through which I received instructions to perform three tasks testing the coordination of my mind, hands, and legs within a specified time limit. Unfortunately, my overall score fell short of qualifying for the PABT, abruptly ending my dream of becoming a pilot. It was very disheartening.

I later came to realise there were many reasons contributing to my performance in the test. Perhaps knowing how to play video games or having taken a mock test for the PABT could have made it easier for me. My preparation felt incomplete, or maybe it was simply fate.

Damcha consoled me, reassuring me that failing the test was not the end of the world, and maybe becoming a pilot was not meant for me. To take my mind off, we explored Varanasi, visiting iconic places like Ganga Ghat, Shri Kashi Vishwanath Temple and other nearby temples. On our return train journey, we saw a very unique sight—a large rainbow visible through the window of the moving train.

It seemed so close that we held out our hands, almost feeling like we could touch it. When we shared this experience with *Ima* later, she explained it was called *chumthang makhong*—a rare sight considered a very auspicious omen.

After his training and induction into the Indian Army, *Damcha* married Sanatombi Sarangthem. Meanwhile, I pursued further studies, completing postgraduation and working towards a doctoral degree (PhD) at Manipur University.

Ima made us understand that as long as we had self-respect and self-esteem, we would be able to live a dignified life. She instilled in us a deep sense of our own value and emphasised the importance of protecting and nurturing our self-worth with utmost care.

Through her life experiences, she learnt the importance of having an insight into people's true intentions. From our early childhood, she imparted this wisdom to us, always keeping a watchful eye on what we did and with whom we mingled. She kept us away from negative influences as we grew older.

We had a diverse group of friends, who visited our home or whom we visited. *Ima* as such was not judgemental, but she could differentiate between true and false friends. She strongly believed in treating everyone, especially friends, with respect and equality. Yet, she also warned us about the presence of some people who might appear patronising or self-serving. These individuals, she cautioned, would never truly be our friends because their primary concern would always be prioritising their own interests above all else.

Ima taught us that true friendship is based on mutual love and affection, where respect is given and received equally. She warned us against those who manipulate friendship for personal gain, urging us to avoid such individuals.

She advised us to be wary of people who appear insincere. While it is impossible to predict anyone's true intentions outright, *Ima* emphasised that true character reveals itself through a few interactions. Drawing from her own experiences, she narrated many instances that underscored the reality that not everyone who posed as friends turned out to be genuine ones.

She also observed the disparity between the rich and the poor, and the status maniacs some people are. She wanted us to understand this division and to recognise those who create barriers. She knew the importance of having genuine friends whom we could rely on, but she aimed to teach us how to distinguish between true and false people—those who genuinely cared for us and would stand by us through our tough times.

Her advice guided us in dealing with different relationships—friendships, romantic relationships, and professional settings. It helped us to develop insight into people's intentions, which is never an easy task. With her words of caution, she helped us to become observant, aiding us in interacting effectively with a diverse range of people and protecting ourselves from those who may cause harm.

Ima herself was very observant. Although she could not read or write, she always used Hindi or English vocabulary in her day-to-day conversations. She learnt by watching television, listening to radio, and interacting with her customers, as well as through our conversations at home. She could orally communicate in Hindi with her Hindi-speaking customers. Since we siblings conversed in English and Hindi at home, in addition to our native language, *Ima* picked up Hindi and English words and phrases from our discussions and used them effectively when needed. She performed calculations mentally during all her sales and dealings with weavers and traders, whereas we mostly relied on our calculators! She practised her elementary arithmetic skills diligently which never failed her in calculations. She was indeed a vibrant learner, always eager to observe and learn.

Baba was also aware of *Ima*'s desire to read and write, so late at night, he used to teach her basic English letters and the Bengali script. During our school days, Bengali script was taught and used instead of *Meitei mayek*, the script of the Manipuri language. *Baba* bought beginner and cursive books for her to practise. *Ima* specifically wanted to learn to write her name, so we taught her to write it in the Bengali script. She went on to sign all her pension, bank transactions and other documents using this script. She told us that she felt a sense of achievement when she was able to do so.

Ima encouraged us to pursue further studies, even when she was financially stressed. When Promila took up research for her doctoral degree, *Ima* was the driving force that propelled my sister to earn her PhD degree. She wished for us to achieve doctoral degrees as if they were her own! Even when I was on the verge of giving up my research work midway, her dreams and encouragement kept me moving to complete it.

Throughout her life, *Ima's* greatest strength was her belief in God and her faith in Him. She often said, "Even in times of loneliness and uncertainty, especially after your father passed away, I persevered with the firm belief that God would always show me my way. His kindness and blessings have enabled me to achieve what I have. Have no fear, for there is an Almighty force that protects and guides us."

She did not lean on others but placed her trust in God. The saying, "God helps those who help themselves" was particularly true for *Ima*—she believed that her hard work and vision would never be in vain because God would always be there to help.

I don't recall her ever treating others poorly—when people treated her unfairly, she would never hold a grudge against them. She would let it go and forgive them, firmly believing that it was not for her to judge, and leaving it to God. It was her firm faith in God and herself that made her our compass. We turned to her for strength, hope, advice, everything else. She fortified us deep within our souls and nurtured us to face challenges. She maintained her connection with God through daily prayers, without fail. Prayer was a quintessential practice in our family—right from waking up in the morning to before going to bed in the evening. *Ima*'s belief was serving God through her hard work. For her, work was worship.

Before *Baba* passed away, *Ima* dedicated herself to organising rituals and prayers every year, as advised by the *kuthi eeba panjis*, the birth chart readers. Since *Baba* was in active service, she feared the risks and dangers he could face while executing his duties. Early in the morning, she would go to renowned *panji*s, carrying *Baba*'s birth chart, and patiently wait until evening if there was a long queue. These rituals and prayers were an annual routine that she meticulously carried out, believing that they would protect *Baba* and our family. However, after *Baba's* demise, she gave up her constant vigil of offering annual prayers and rituals, feeling that everyone was vulnerable and life was uncertain. She did not lose faith in God but surrendered to His plans for us. She let go her reliance on birth charts and rituals, focusing more on her inner connection with God through daily prayers, which gave her strength to work, fulfil her duties, and maintain her empathy towards others.

Nevertheless, *Ima* continued to worship Meitei deities during festivals, such as *Lai Haraoba*—an annual festival for Meiteis to perform rituals to appease local deities; the Kang Rath Yatra—

similar to the procession held in Puri (Odisha), celebrating the journey of Lord Jagannath with his sister Subhadra and brother Balabhadra in a giant *rath* (chariot) pulled by Vaishnavite Meitei devotees; *Saroi Khangba*—when *lamta thangja* offerings are made on the Saturdays in March to appease spirits through the food offerings and to ward off evil spirits; *Sankranti*—dedicated to the sun deity; *Imoinu Iratpa*—where offerings of fish and rice are made to Goddess *Imoinu* to seek her blessings; *Sajibu Cheiraoba*—the Meitei New Year festival, and Diwali, among others. In the spirit of these festivals and what they signified, *Ima* always believed in God's providence and His guidance.

Behind all our accomplishments lay a long struggle and the unwavering support, conviction, and prayers of our dear *Ima.* Every night and throughout the days, her thoughts were centred on us—our lives and our futures. Every success, every milestone we reached was her victory, her achievement, for which she always expressed deep gratitude.

9

Lighter Moments

Ima lived in every moment to the best of her ability, and that's how we learnt to do the same. She took care of her health through regular exercise and morning walks. In addition to exercises, what really nourished her soul was music. She loved listening to the radio and needed it by her side almost all the time. She listened to old melodies, both Hindi and Manipuri, forgotten by the present generation, such as the old Manipuri song rendered by the singer, composer, and lyricist, Nongmaithem Pahari, which voiced the singer's melancholy and touched the listener's heart:

Nangna leini, eina meini

Nangna thamoi, eina meichak

Nangna mitlu, eina pirang

Nangna houba, eina loiba.

(You are a flower, I am the fire

You are the beating heart; I am the pain.

You are the eye, I am the tears

You are the beginning and I am the end.)

Another Manipuri song, sung by Ningthoujam Nabachandra, the famous Manipuri artiste known for his melodious voice, that *Ima* loved hearing was:

Tum tum tum tum khongli uthum na,

Tamna tamna yeiri khongthang na,

Louri yalliba khungi pakhang,

Humang na tup tup tare.

(*The bird, Uthum is chirping tum tum tum tum,*

An echo is reverberating over a long distance,

Village youths cutting the paddy in the field,

Are perspiring drop by drop.)

She would listen to these lovely melodies on the radio while lying in bed. She had started listening to the radio more frequently after *Baba*'s demise. She said, "I feel better when I hear music. Even if I am not actually listening, it somehow helps distract me from my stress and burdens." Songs played on the radio in the background while she did her work and household chores. She even started taking her radio to *Ima Keithel* to listen with her friends to radio dramas aired at noon. And she would end her day listening to more music before going to bed.

After her day's work, she used to relax by watching television after dinner. She enjoyed watching Hindi movies or serials, Manipuri movies, Korean serials, and *Shumang Leela*s—the Manipuri outdoor theatre dramas telecast on our local channel. *Gadar Ek Prem Katha* was one of her favourite Hindi movies and *Nongallabasu Thaballei Manam* was the Manipuri movie she could never have enough of. Her favourite Korean dramas were *Autumn in My Heart* and *Stairway to Heaven*. We used to read the subtitles to her.

Loving and kind, *Ima* was a selfless person who always thought of others before herself. Everyone she worked with—her weavers, business contacts, relatives, and acquaintances—loved her because she empathised with them and connected on a personal level. She shared her stories with them and listened to theirs, offering help in every possible way. For our relatives, she was someone they would turn to for advice or discussion. Her maternal relatives fondly called her *Inecha, Idomcha*, and *Bobok Memcha* (Aunt, Granny).

Ima formed a close bond with most of her weavers and regularly visited them at their work sheds in their homes. I vividly remember when a tribal woman came to our house asking for clothes. *Ima* generously gave her some, and from then on, they shared a warm relationship. Mangai, the tribal woman, began visiting regularly to meet *Ima*, always bringing fruits or vegetables she grew at home. They would sit down, share a cup of tea and snacks, and enjoy chatting. *Ima* never underestimated or disrespected anyone, which likely contributed to why people revered and loved her.

I cleared the Manipur Civil Service examination in 2012, and my first posting was as a sub-divisional officer (SDO) at Patsoi in the Imphal West district. Since I was entitled to a government vehicle, I would drop *Ima* at *Ima Keithel* on my way to office, and we would return together in the evening. Soon, she began sharing a small portion of whatever she bought, such as fruits, vegetables or fish, with my driver. She would ask about his family, and they would engage in conversation, showing her unique love for fellow beings and her readiness to reach out to them. She often told us, "Treat people with respect, show sympathy, empathise with them, and they will reciprocate in kind." Her acts of helping others in need and her humanity brought love, happiness, and respect to her. She did not waste time worrying unnecessarily because she believed in taking action and being brave and bold.

She repeatedly advised us never to harbour ill feelings, anger, or resentment. She would say, "Even if others say or do bad things to you, you need not be like them. If you try to behave like them, you stoop to their level. I chose to forgive those who hurt my sentiments, and I felt a weight lift off me by letting go."

Ima tried not to dwell on any hurt or pain she suffered, diluting her problems by letting go. She immersed herself in what gave her hope—her children, her grandchildren, her work, and her love for humanity. She showed us that through forgiveness and love, we could conquer any negativity that confronted us.

She loved her grandchildren immensely, with all her heart. In total, there were a dozen of them—Angelina, Priyobrata, Melvin, Parambir, Harris, Derek, Zoshuan, Priyadarshini, Steve, Stacia, Roshni, and Machanghen.[1] She would host lunch for all of us at home, and these occasions became days of complete family reunion. She loved watching her grandsons and granddaughters play on our front verandah, relishing the noise and laughter, and the warmth of family closeness.

---

1 Altogether, Ima had 14 grandchildren. Yailen and Mitlu were born after her passing. Sadly, her grandchild Harris passed away in 2023.

Tirth Mapan

Another thing *Ima* loved was going on trips to religious sites and temples, such as the occasional *tirth mapan* and annual Buddha Purnima trips. It gave her peace of mind and renewed her soul, as she carried pure devotion in her heart. She also took us on these trips. One such *tirth mapan* was arranged by the people in our locality when we were young. Let me take you on the journey we had.

The *tirth mapan* was meant to cover nine religious sites—Bijoy Govinda temple, Shree Shree Govindajee temple, Ramji Prabhu temple, Kaina temple, Thongam Mondum, Ibudhou Thangjing temple of Moirang, Gopinath temple, Abdieta temple, and Hiyanthang Lairembi. It was a day-long trip, accompanied by families from our locality. I remember *Ima* was wearing a *pumngou phanek*, a pale pink traditional sarong with a white *inaphee*. She applied *chandan* on her nose in an elongated diamond shape. She also dressed us in white shirts and *pumngouphanek*s and applied *chandan* on our noses after bathing us.

The trip started early in the morning around 7 a.m. She took her time packing items like flowers, incense sticks, candles, coins, banana leaves, and other essentials for offering prayers. Our first stop was the serene Bijoy Govinda temple in Sagolband, Imphal West, known for its domes and wall carvings of elephants, flowers, and leaves. It is dedicated to the elder brother of Shree Govindajee.

Next, we headed to the Shree Shree Govindajee temple located at Wangkhei, in the Palace Compound (next to the palace of the former Manipuri kings), Imphal East. The Govindajee temple is the most visited temple by Vaishnavite devotees in Manipur. It is a pristine white temple with golden twin domes where Lord Krishna (Lord Govind), Goddess Radha, Lord Balaram, Lord Jagannath,

Lord Balabhadra, and Goddess Subhadra are worshipped. This temple holds the distinction of being the largest Vaishnava temple in Imphal and serves as a symbol of devotion, upholding its historical and spiritual significance for thousands of devotees who come to offer prayers.

Ima always looked forward to visiting the Govindajee temple and took us there frequently on occasions such as *Krishna Janmasthami.* Although our indigenous religion is Sanamahism, our parents embraced Vaishnava culture and traditions, including the worship of our presiding local deities. As a result, we were exposed to both Vaishnavism and Sanamahism. Our parents were both secular and believed in an Almighty God who protected us. *Ima* had gained spiritual knowledge in her youth by listening to oral recitals of the *Bhagavad Gita* in her Brahmin neighbourhood. She passed down her knowledge to us, teaching us everything she knew. Therefore, we observed all occasions, prayers, and rituals of Vaishnavism, and offering prayers at temples was a customary practice for our family. On this trip, she offered her prayers with closed eyes, kneeling with her hands held together and palms slightly open. After chanting her prayers, she bowed her head. We imitated whatever she did, following her as she walked three times around Shree Shree Govindajee temple before returning to our bus seats.

The bus then headed to the next religious site known as Ramji Prabhu, located at Wangkhei Ningthem Pukhri Mapal in the Imphal East district. In this old temple, idols of Lord Rama are worshipped. Everyone alighted from the bus and entered the temple premises to offer prayers. *Ima* showed us the Ningthem *pukhri*, a pond spanning a hundred fathoms in front of the temple gate. It was so large that we could not see the faces of people on the other side. The cool breeze from it refreshed everyone and brought a sense of peace after the prayer offerings.

Our next destination was Kaina, a picturesque hillock where the Kaina temple was perched. *Ima* told us that Shree Govindajee had once instructed the Manipuri king, Maharaja Bhagyachandra, in his dream to build a place of worship in Kaina, enshrined with his image carved out of a holy jackfruit tree growing on the hillock. Since then, the Vaishnavites consider Kaina a holy place. We reached there by noon, exhausted after the long ride. After completing our prayer offerings, we rested under the big *mandap* (raised porch) of the Kaina temple. The organisers had arranged lunch there, and it was a perfect location surrounded by green hills and fields stretching at the foothills of Kaina. The peaceful environment and beauty of the temple renewed everyone's energy.

After Kaina, our bus headed to Thongam Mondum located on the Mondum *ching*. *Ima* led us while climbing the footsteps of the Mondum Hill, which was very tiring. We offered our prayers and threw coins towards the huge stone, believed to be a Shiva idol, while the priest continuously poured milk over it. There was a huge rush at all these religious sites because *tirth mapan*s are usually organised on auspicious days like *Buddha Purnima,* when devotees throng temples. *Ima* held our hands tightly, fearing that we would get lost in the crowd. After descending Mondum *ching*, we searched for our bus. By then, it was afternoon and our trip was almost halfway done.

Everyone was summoned for the next religious site, dedicated to Ibudhou Thangjing of Moirang, the most popular sylvan god in Manipur and significant in Meitei mythology. Ibudhou Thangjing is considered one of the eight gods who guard the directions, specifically the southwest of Manipur. We offered our prayers for peace, protection, and prosperity at the ancient temple dedicated to this pre-Hindu deity. The temple, renowned for its exquisite carvings and beautiful architecture, has a large *mandap*, and a compound where Moirang *Lai Haroaba* is celebrated every year in May. By then, the sun had set.

The journey from Moirang to Kwakeithel took one hour. In Bishnupur, the bus made quick stops at the Gopinath temple of Ningthoukhong and the Abdieta temple of Lamangdong, both dedicated to Lord Krishna. It was almost dark by this time. At the Bishnupur bazaar, everyone got down and *Ima* bought *soibum* (fermented bamboo shoots) and a special stone mortar and pestle made by locals of Bishnupur. The organisers announced that the last religious site would be Hiyangthang Lairembi temple, but due to the darkness and lateness of the hour, we did not make a stop there. As we passed the Hiyangthang Lairembi temple, *Ima* told us to close our eyes and pray in our hearts. We did not feel disappointed about missing the last religious site because *Ima* had already taken us there a couple of times earlier on *bor numit*, the third day of Durga Puja. It was a temple complex on a hillock, dedicated to Goddess Hiyangthang Lairembi. It was majestic with an aura of tranquillity. We reached home at around 7.30 p.m., wrapping up the day's trip peacefully.

Ningol Chakkouba

Another special occasion for *Ima* was *Ningol Chakkouba*, a celebration devoted to married Manipuri women who are invited by their maternal families, particularly by their parents and brothers, for a grand lunch. After the feast, the parents and brothers give gifts, mainly traditional clothes like *phanek*s and *inaphee*s, to their married daughters and sisters. It is celebrated in November on the second day in the lunar month of *Hiyangei*. *Ningol Chakkouba* strengthens the bond between sisters and brothers. We eagerly awaited this festival, which *Ima* particularly loved because it rekindled her ties with her maternal home. A few days before the festival, *Ima*'s elder brother would come to our home to invite her for *Ningol Chakkouba*. He would bring a betel leaf with areca nuts wrapped in a banana leaf, which serves as a formal invitation. At the same time, *Baba* and our uncles would invite our aunt Tolen and her daughters for a *Ningol Chakkouba* lunch at our home. The entire family would rejuvenate in the festive mood.

To prepare for the feast, *Ima* and Promila used to catch prawns floating on the surface of our pond, located on the easternmost side of our house, using a *polang* (bamboo basket) or an *innjao* (fishing net). Then, a day before *Ningol Chakkouba*, all the men in our family, including our brothers, Uncle Gokul, and cousins, would drain the water from the pond and catch the fish by using a *longhop* (a fish trap), a *long* (bamboo spear with an array of pointed bamboo fingers), and sometimes with their bare hands. We would clap and cheer every time a big fish was caught. The fish were collected in a *khudeng* and taken to the kitchen where preparations, such as cutting vegetables, potatoes, tomatoes, herbs, garlic, onions, chillies, and other ingredients, would go on till late in the night at our home under the light emitted by large hurricane lanterns. There was much laughter and gaiety in anticipation of *Ningol Chakkouba*.

Ima would dress up in Meitei traditional attire, wearing a *mapannaibi phanek* and a silk *inaphee* for the day, looking beautiful and elegant as always. We also got new dresses every year for the occasion. *Baba* would buy fruit, mainly apples, oranges, coconuts, and bananas, along with other edibles, which *Ima* would stack in a basket. November was usually very cold and foggy in the early morning. However, this never stopped us from bathing in the cold morning. While we waited for the thick fog to clear up, *Ima* would apply glycerine mixed with a little water on our hands and feet. She would hold our chins and comb our hair, neatly parting it in two halves after applying hair oil. The sunshine would come out much later.

and *Ima* never missed her offerings to Lord Jagannath throughout her life.

Passing Out Parade (POP)

When *Damcha* was selected for the Indian Army after his graduation, he proceeded for his training at the Officers Training Academy (OTA) in Chennai. Every year, as part of OTA tradition, a Passing Out Parade (POP) was held for the newly commissioned officers at the end of their training. It was a proud moment for *Ima*, and I was fortunate to accompany her to attend this important event. The visit to Chennai with *Ima* is one of my cherished memories because I could spend time with her and share in the joy of witnessing *Damcha* being commissioned in the army.

Everyone was apprehensive about both of us going on the journey to Chennai, but they need not have worried because *Ima* was fearless and travelling was not new to her. I was in my first year semester of the Master's programme and had already made a couple of trips outside Manipur to places like Guwahati, Bangalore (now Bengaluru), and Varanasi. I had gone to Bangalore during my NCC days for the Vayu Sainik Camp, so travelling south was not entirely unfamiliar.

We took a flight from Imphal to Kolkata, where David, a cousin of *Damcha*'s friend Seiminlin, received us at the airport. Seiminlin's parents had offered to help us when they learnt that we were going to Chennai via Kolkata and were kind enough to inform David. It turned out to be a pleasant surprise as David and one of his friends accompanied us to Howrah railway station. The four of us enjoyed a hearty meal of Bengali fish curry and rice, with a spectacular view of the Howrah Bridge and the small tourist boats floating in the wide Hooghly River. After our meal, we headed to our railway terminal, where they helped us with our luggage. At the platform, we had to wait for about three to four hours for the train.

During our long wait, I noticed a young man staring at us curiously. He then asked us in Manipuri where we were going. We were surprised—from his appearance, we had never imagined he knew Manipuri! The mystery was solved when he introduced himself as Sadasivan, a Keralite who had settled in Manipur. He mentioned his train was scheduled an hour later than ours, and we gladly engaged in conversation to pass the time. Sadasivan also assisted us in finding our seats when our train arrived, initiating our day-and-a-half journey to Chennai.

Ima enjoyed watching the landscape from the window and talked to our fellow travellers, using the bits of Hindi she knew. The passengers were from all over India—Bengal, the south, and even Sikkim. We reached Chennai in the early morning, and R.K. Somio, *Damcha*'s friend, came to receive us.

The OTA has a sprawling campus at St. Thomas Mount, Chennai. We were escorted to *Damcha*'s room and were excited to see him. After strolling around the campus, we headed to the cafeteria, quickly ate our meal and resumed exploring the OTA grounds. When we peeked at the parade rehearsal, *Ima* beamed with pride as we observed the practice session, especially watching *Damcha* on the big parade ground. A born leader since childhood, *Damcha* won the hearts of people wherever he went, and we could see he had the same effect there.

On 22 September 2007, the Parameswaran Drill Square at the OTA in Chennai witnessed a spectacle that left an incredibly strong impression on the parents and attendees alike. It marked the POP for the SS-84 (NT) and WSE -30 Course, a momentous day culminating 49 weeks of rigorous and unforgiving training for 252 cadets, including 69 women cadets. My brother, Lieutenant Tiken Oinam, achieved the coveted appointment of Senior Under Officer (SUO) commanding the parade contingent of the Jessami Company in the Ranjit Battalion. As *Ima* and I looked on, we were filled with a mix of emotions—pride, joy, and perhaps a bit of nervousness. His journey to becoming an officer and the SUO was undoubtedly the result of hard work and dedication. The rigorous training at the OTA tested the limits of physical endurance, mental fortitude, and leadership skills. The POP was the culmination of this journey, showcasing the transformation of cadets into disciplined and confident officers.

The Parameswaran Drill Square, bathed in the golden hues of a September morning, became the stage for this grand display of military prowess. Lieutenant Tiken Oinam, wielding a majestic sword, led the parade contingent of the Jessami Company in the Ranjit Battalion, issuing unwavering commands in his strong voice. The atmosphere brimmed with energy as the cadets, now transformed into poised officers, executed precise drill movements under his leadership. His role commanded respect, and every action reflected the discipline and precision instilled during the gruelling training period. As he marched ahead, his posture exuded confidence, and the gleam of the sword reflected countless hours of training. The parade itself was a display of military discipline: synchronised movements, the crisp sound of marching boots, and the glint of polished uniforms created a mesmerising spectacle. Pride and anticipation filled the air as parents, family members, and friends observed their loved ones being elevated to commissioned officers.

When Lieutenant Tiken Oinam was announced as the Parade Commander, it was a moment of pride for the Oinam family.

Witnessing my brother's commanding presence at the parade filled us with immense fulfilment. His role as the SUO was more than ceremonial; it signified a high level of leadership and responsibility. He has not only earned a title but also the respect of his peers and superiors. The POP that September day was more than a military ceremony; it was a celebration of resilience, determination, and the pursuit of excellence. As the parade concluded, the newly commissioned officers stood tall, ready to embark on their respective journeys in the service of the nation.

Parents were honoured with the opportunity to place the insignia of two five-pointed stars, signifying the rank of "Lieutenant", on their children's uniforms. Full of emotions, I watched *Ima* place the insignia on *Damcha*'s shoulders. On the day of the POP, she wore a half saree paired with our traditional *mapannaibi phanek* and an off-white Rani *phee*. The POP marked the beginning of Lieutenant Tiken Oinam's promising career dedicated to serving the nation with honour and integrity.

Laishram Chaoba, a Manipuri woman officer, also graduated that day, and her family attended the POP as well. Somio was also present with one of his friends, and we had a hearty dinner party.

The day after the POP, we went sightseeing and visited beaches and malls. We also tried south Indian food, which was different from our Meitei style of cooking, so *Ima* managed with rice and dal. On the third day, we left the OTA.

On our return journey, just before boarding the train, a shocking incident occurred. While on the railway platform, an overweight Tamil man suddenly collapsed right in front of us. He was pulling a cart and was accompanied by a lady. People rushed to assist him, but later we heard that he had died from a heart attack. It was a terribly sad incident, leaving us speechless and helpless, and reminding us once again of life's fragility. By evening, our train journey began, and after our flight from Kolkata, we returned to Imphal.

Chakrata and the Taj Trip

Towards the end of 2014, my niece Angelina, *Ima*, and I packed up for a short holiday trip to Delhi and Dehradun, a journey we had specially planned for *Ima*.

Our first destination was Chakrata, where *Damcha* was posted as an army major, via Delhi. *Damcha* had kept his car in Delhi, and from there, he drove us to his place of posting. It was a long drive from Delhi to Dehradun via Haryana, approximately 250 kilometres. We admired the green and golden fields of Haryana, a breath-taking sight with the setting sun casting its softening light on the landscape. During the journey, we stopped at *dhaba*s (roadside eateries) to savour local *chai*, *samosa*s, fruits, and other treats. The road to Dehradun was mostly flat, but from there, it became winding as we ascended towards Chakrata.

Chakrata, a cantonment town in Dehradun district, sits at an altitude of 7000 feet above sea level. By the time we arrived at 10 p.m., we had already missed seeing the deep gorges. *Damcha*'s caretaker had thoughtfully lit a fire in the fireplace, providing instant warmth from the cold outside. It was December, nearing New Year's Eve. We only realised the depth and danger of the gorges on our return journey in daylight. Some stretches of the road had no protective guard rails, with the sheer drop uncomfortably close.

Early in the morning in Chakrata, *Ima* opened the window in our bedroom to take in the stunning view of the snow-clad mountains and dense green trees. I too glanced out to admire the lush greenery and snowy peaks. The coniferous trees, thickly spread across the nearby mountain slopes, stood in their natural beauty. After breakfast, we leisurely soaked up the sun, free from responsibilities and worries. At home, *Ima* was often concerned about our future, but here, *Damcha* and I wanted to see her smile and bring her happiness. And this was the perfect place where we found peace and solace.

We explored the Buddhist stupas atop the mountains, where we revelled in the tranquillity. Our next stops included the bustling Chakrata market, known for its handicrafts and street food, and the stunning Tiger Falls cascading down a mountain. Enjoying the snowy weather, Angelina and I played in the white snow. Back at *Damcha*'s quarters, we savoured Sikkimese momos on New Year's Eve. *Ima* also had a quick health check-up at his army station. Later, we went shopping in Dehradun and watched the popular Bollywood movie *PK*, starring Aamir Khan.

The day before we departed from Chakrata, *Damcha*'s commanding officer, a South Indian gentleman with a delightful mother, wife, and two charming young daughters, invited us to dinner. *Ima* and I enjoyed their company and felt comfortable in their presence.

It was time for us to depart from Chakrata. In the morning, we headed back to Delhi and arrived by afternoon. After having snacks and refreshments at Connaught Place, we rested for a while before continuing our journey to Agra via the Yamuna Expressway. The drive along the expressway was enjoyable as there was no congestion or overtaking; every driver kept to their lanes. *Ima,* as usual, kept a vigil while *Damcha* drove, reminding him to be careful. We arrived in Agra late at night, and stayed at the Agra army cantonment.

Ima woke us up early in the morning, and during our stroll around the army campus, we saw many beautiful peacocks. With *Damcha* as our guide, we toured the cantonment. Every moment was precious; the smiles on *Ima*'s face lit up our hearts with happiness. Her radiant smile and the morning rays that shone behind her while we took her photographs will stay forever in my memories.

Afterwards, we headed to the Taj Mahal in a *tonga*. Private vehicles were directed to a parking area and were not allowed to proceed further. As we entered through the pathway leading to the main gateway of the Taj Mahal with our tickets, we admired the Taj gardens with fountains and pools of clear water. The white, majestic Taj Mahal, resplendent in its charm and splendour, stood tall right in front of us.

A particularly delightful sight for us was the large *amla*s (Indian gooseberries) in the Taj gardens. In Manipur, *amla*s are very small, so these ones delighted us, and we collected some from the garden.

Photographs were taken by local photographers at the Taj Mahal. Since shoes were not allowed inside, we left ours outside and wore the white booties provided. We could feel the heat of the marble floor beneath the thin booties. During our tour of the Taj Mahal, we saw the tomb of Mumtaz Mahal inside the mausoleum. After concluding our tour and exiting through the gate, the photographer quickly approached us with the photographs in which we were grinning as much as we could! We purchased Taj Mahal mementos and other handicrafts from the stalls. *Ima* said, "I'm glad we came to see the Taj Mahal," words that filled us with delight.

After returning from Agra, we did some shopping in Delhi, before flying back to Imphal.

These are just a few instances of *Ima*'s lighter moments, when she could briefly forget her worries. Despite life's relentless struggles, she embraced these happy moments and appreciated the beauty along her journey. She lived in the present and valued what was meaningful, and I treasure my memories of her positive outlook.

10

A Friend, Philosopher, and Guide

When I was a child, my first encounter with the fear of death happened in a dream. I dreamed that *Ima* was attacked by a thief with a knife, leaving her hands bruised and her skin peeled off. It was such a horrifying nightmare that I woke up in tears. Throughout the day, I couldn't stop thinking about death and how painful it could be. The idea of losing my parents terrified me deeply, but with time, this fear subsided. Nevertheless, it made me realise how precious she was to me and how daunting and final death could be.

When I was a toddler, *Ima* used to extinguish the light on our *mangol* (front porch) and carry me on her back to lull me to sleep, singing the lullaby,

Tha tha thabungton!

Nacha morambi pobige pobi sanam nambige,

Heibong charong amatang thadabirak u thabungton!

Tha tha thabungton.

(O Moon! youngest of your kin,

Let me carry my beloved on my back,

Drop a bunch of fig fruit, O Moon!

O Moon! youngest of your kin.)

I was deeply attached to her and would follow her around most of the time. Being the youngest child, I enjoyed certain privileges. She would take me everywhere she went, whether to the nearby grocery store, her weavers' houses, or her maternal home, always holding my hand as we walked. I felt secure and believed it was my right to accompany her wherever she went. I would listen intently to conversations with her weavers and mundane stories shared by our relatives. During my early school days, she walked me to my *balwadi* (preschool) centre and carried me on her back through flooded *leirak*s in Mayaikoibi on rainy days. A sense of completeness, warmth, happiness, and security was always associated with her.

We would talk about anything and everything. Sometimes, she would recount stories from her youth, about our father, about the difficult periods she had faced, and her moments of joy. In turn, I would share my dreams for the future, about my friends, my worries, and problems. She was never judgemental and patiently listened to everything I had to say, no matter how trivial. She helped me understand that experiencing ups and downs in friendships, relationships, and facing failures was normal. She would then narrate her own experiences, to teach me the importance of courage in overcoming setbacks and seizing new opportunities. Talking to her and seeking her advice always made me feel better when I had to make important decisions.

I would often bombard her with questions, especially when I felt agitated with myself and others. She was always patient with me.

She would tell me, "*Waa ngangbada tin yotharaga nganggadabani, thabak toubada munna khantharaga tougadabani* which means, 'Always think carefully before you speak and only take action after thinking the matter through'.

"If you want to become a wise person, you should be careful with your words. A word means a lot. It can build or destroy relationships, it can save lives, and it can inspire. It has the power to shape a person's destiny. The words we speak reflect our level of thinking. The answers to all your questions lie within you. You should be able to reflect and contemplate on the questions in your mind. There is no definite answer to why people behave a certain way, but it is certainly influenced by their level of thinking and thought processes," she would say, imparting her wisdom.

She would emphasise, "Bem, you should nurture love through the use of right words within your family, in your relationships, in your friendships, and in your conduct."

She was a friend, philosopher, and guide to me as I grew up. We would often sit on our verandah after dinner or take walks, chatting about different aspects of life, our faces turned towards the night breeze.

One day, I asked *Ima* if she knew about Manipuri dance. She replied confidently, "Of course." I told her I was finding it difficult to learn the steps of *Leima Jagoi* and asked her to teach me. *Leima Jagoi* is a traditional dance of the Meitei community in Manipur. I did not have dancing skills and struggled to make graceful moves. She patiently taught me the dance steps in a simple manner, emphasising that I needed to relax my body completely and give in to the gentle movements of the fingers and the feet.

"The subtle body movements come with a calm mind. *Leima Jagoi* and the essence of Manipuri dance are about peacefulness, delicate foot movements and tender hand gestures," she explained, demonstrating the basic steps. First, she lightly stepped forward with her right foot, followed by the left foot and a slight bend of the left knee. As both her knees bent, her fingers moved, turning the right palm inside towards her body, while the left palm faced outward and her head tilted slightly to the right. Slowly, she raised her left knee and moved her left foot backwards followed by the right foot, gradually releasing her curled fingers. It was a moonlight dance lesson that night. I practised the basic steps with her, and *Ima* corrected my footwork, hand gestures, head tilt, and knee bends. Over time, my movements became more graceful, boosting my confidence when performing *Leima Jagoi* and other Manipuri dance forms during my school and NCC days.

Nowadays, almost every child starts riding a tricycle or bicycle at a very young age. I, however, learnt to ride a bicycle late during my school days. All my older siblings knew how to ride, so it was inevitable that I would learn too. *Ima* would wake me up early in the morning for practice sessions when the roads were clear of vehicles. We had a bicycle with the brand name Captain, which had passed through all my siblings before reaching me. Standing by my side, *Ima* gave instructions as I took my first few steps with the bicycle. I tried to position my legs on both sides of the bicycle, with my feet near the pedals, and attempted to peddle with the left foot first, then my right, as the cycle started moving. I pushed the cycle along, taking a few steps with the pedals. Balancing the bicycle seemed like an impossible task—it took many days of practice. *Ima* kept monitoring my progress day after day, even when there was no improvement over several weeks.

Eventually, I started riding short distances, and completing those first few rounds while seated on the bicycle seat filled me with excitement and a sense of accomplishment. This short-distance practice, under *Ima*'s watchful eye, went on for several days. Then came the fateful moment. As I began cycling a longer distance, I suddenly saw vehicles approaching and grew nervous. I lost control and fell right into a pile of dumped garbage on the roadside. Though I suffered some scratches, I managed to get back on my feet.

Ima congratulated me, saying, "You can't learn to ride a bicycle without a few falls." Soon, I learnt to ride confidently without fear of falling. While it may not seem like a big achievement, I owe my ability to ride a bicycle to *Ima*'s encouragement and her regular practice sessions with me. She wanted us to be independent, and learning to ride a bicycle meant we could manage our daily transportation needs. We rode our bicycles to school and to tuition classes by ourselves.

During my college days, I joined the National Cadets Corps (NCC). I used to be captivated by the camp stories *Damcha* shared after returning from his NCC camps. Initially, *Ima* was apprehensive about me joining the NCC because of the strenuous physical activities involved, but I convinced her that I would learn a lot. Finally, she agreed. I enrolled in No.1 Squadron, Senior Air Wing NCC Unit, Imphal, as an air wing cadet. For air wing cadets like me, participating in the Vayu Sainik Camp was the ultimate dream. When I joined the NCC, there was a ban on NCC activities in Manipur due to the insurgency movement. As a result, we had to train indoors for entry into the Vayu Sainik Camp, as we were unable to practice in an open playground.

The pre-camp selection for the Vayu Sainik Camp was held at Guwahati, where I was one of the eight girls chosen; the rest, about 12, were boys. Only four girls would be selected for final training at the Vayu Sainik Camp in Bangalore, so I knew I had to give my all to achieve my goal. Despite the tough competition, we bonded through our practice sessions, cultural programmes, group songs and dances, and even punishments. Physically and emotionally drained during the camp, none of us were sure about being selected.

Back then, there were only Public Call Offices (PCOs), not the mobile connectivity we have today. With no PCO at our camp area, we could only make phone calls home during evening outings. One day, I felt restless and needed to call *Ima*. I requested our associate NCC officer (ANO), Madam Rejubala, who had a mobile handset, to let me make a call, and she agreed. When *Ima* came on the line, I started telling her about my tension and anxiety, but halfway through, I broke down crying. She understood what I was going through and listened patiently. Calmly, she said, "Why are you crying? Why are you so disheartened? It's not important whether you get selected or not; what matters is you are there and enjoying your camp." Her words instantly lifted my spirits and relieved the pressure I felt. I was able to control my emotions and regain my focus. Fortunately, I was selected for the Vayu Sainik Camp in Bangalore too.

Throughout my struggles, *Ima* was always there to provide encouragement, dedicating her time and resources to support my studies. She stood by me through all my personal turmoil, emotional upheavals, struggles in studies, friendships, infatuations and heartbreaks. More than a mother, *Ima* was a true friend to me, always reiterating her commitment to stand by me through life's challenges. I saw the hardships *Ima* had to experience in the past and knew how desperately she wanted us to steer clear of such circumstances in our lives.

After graduating, I pursued postgraduate studies in Life Sciences and continued with research at the university. At that time, autorickshaw services became popular, and *Ima* and I commuted together in these three-wheelers. Every *leikai* had one or two autorickshaws plying to *Ima Keithel.* Autorickshaws were available near our locality, starting from Kuraomakhong just a short distance from our house to *Ima Keithel. Ima* would head to her *potpham* at *Laxmi Keithel* while I would go on to Manipur University. After classes or research, I would help her to tie the big bag containing her shawls with two long ropes crossing diagonally from each side. Once she placed them in her stall, we would go back home together. When alone, she managed to tie them herself, though it required great strength to secure the ropes tightly, which I never managed to do. Vendors in the market preferred to keep their products in stalls and would pay a minimal fee to a group of persons who looked after the goods.

Amid the bustling chatter and noise of the crowd, I always found peace whenever I sat with *Ima* in her stall. We often indulged in hot *samosas* from Jalpaan Hotel, paired with the quintessential *chai* served in small glasses. Adjacent to Brightways, a clothing boutique, stood a sweet shop in Thangal Bazaar where we savoured her favourite *rasmalai*—a tender, mouth-melting dessert, expertly shaped into perfect rounds and garnished with almond sprinkles. She also loved smoked fish, especially *kandla*, *rohu*, and *ngamu leirou*. It became her routine to buy something daily as per necessity. I learnt her knack for selecting fresh vegetables and fruits based on their appearance, familiarised myself with market rates, and learnt to discern inflated rates across various commodities, be it food or clothes. Every shopping excursion with her was a delightful experience.

Ima made an effort to support me during my preparation for competitive examinations. My intensive preparation for the civil services examination began after my Master's degree while pursuing my doctoral degree. I joined coaching classes at Vision IAS Study

Circle in Nagamapal. She always ensured that I had enough time to study. She would wake me up early in the morning because the coaching classes started at around 6 a.m. Food for me was already cooked by 5.30 a.m., and she would pack it in a tiffin carrier before going to *Ima Keithel.* She also went to *Ima Keithel* early. I would carry the tiffin carrier to my coaching class, then took it to Manipur University where I ate my lunch in my laboratory before starting my research work. This arrangement saved time. Sometimes she would bring my tiffin to *Ima Keithel,* and I would collect it from her after my coaching class before heading to Manipur University.

Ima Keithel was undergoing renovation during those days, so *Ima* had to sit in the temporary market with tin roofing that heated up under the summer sun, making the stalls unbearably hot. But she carried on as it was her dream to see us study at the highest level—she always believed she could have achieved more if she had been educated. She often remarked, "If I could read and write, my life would have been different. I would have accomplished much more. I wish I could write about my life, my journey with its hardships and joys, and the experiences I have had."

In the quiet moments before we retired to sleep, *Ima* and I used to reflect on our lives. Usually, she would switch on her radio while lying flat on the bed, her head resting on the pillow. As she gazed blankly at the ceiling, I would either be reading a book on my bed or silently reminiscing about the day's events with my eyes closed. Bedtime became the ideal time to release all the pent-up emotions, stress, and tension by sharing them with *Ima.* She would also share her thoughts and plans, trying to sort out one by one the many things she had on her mind. Whether it was concerns about her financial problems and sales at *Ima Keithel,* or worries about our lives and relatives, talking about what bothered us made everything seem simpler and more manageable.

Finally, she would say, "Everything will turn out well; there's no need to think too much about a problem. We should do what has to be done and leave the rest to God." The Almighty was her source of strength. She prayed to keep her stress and tensions at bay, and advised me to do the same.

Sometimes, we would talk late into the night, deeply immersed in her memories. She recounted a tale about a woman from her neighbourhood, describing it in her own words: "There was a married woman in our locality who was a very talented singer. She conducted herself admirably as an obedient daughter-in-law, always showing deep respect to her elders. Whenever she entered through the gate and saw them sitting on the front porch, she would remove her shoes, and cover her head with her *inaphee* before proceeding inside. She was a very hard-working person, singing during the day to earn her livelihood and managing all household chores as a homemaker. She aspired to educate herself further, yearning for more knowledge, yet she had no time for her studies. Nevertheless, she did not give up on her dreams. After finishing her daily household chores, she started attending night classes at a local school. After passing her final exams, she enrolled in college, again continuing with night classes. With determination and perseverance, she completed her school and college education. Later, she secured a government job, which was highly commendable. I admired this graceful lady and how she achieved her goals through hard work and a never-say-die attitude."

This lady was an inspiration to *Ima*, and she respected her a lot not just for her accomplishments but also for her adherence to Meitei customs. In our Meitei tradition, it's customary to remove shoes before entering a house and to cover the head before elder male relatives, especially in-laws, as a sign of respect. *Ima* herself followed these traditions. She advised me to appreciate the beauty in the customs passed down by our forefathers.

She said, "The respect you show to your traditions reflects the good upbringing you have. They should not be forsaken, and you should aspire to follow such customs that demonstrate respect. You should strive to balance both your family and work, just as this lady did in her life."

I listened intently to *Ima*, absorbing every word she said.

In 2008, the year I completed my Master's degree, I sat for my first preliminary examination for the Manipur Civil Services. The preliminary examination went well, but it was later cancelled. The results were not declared due to a delay or error in conducting the examination. I had decided to continue my research work and pursue a career in teaching or appear for the Indian Forest Service Examination. I continued my preparations.

Meanwhile, the notification for the Manipur Civil Services Examination came again in 2010, and I appeared for the preliminary examination. The government had decided to conduct the examination as there had been a ban on recruitment in the state for quite some time. Recruitment is not conducted annually but based on necessity, following approval from the state cabinet to lift the recruitment ban. Thus, the recruitment process itself took time. The results were announced, and I successfully cleared the prelims.

Next came the tougher main examinations. I had chosen two optional subjects, Zoology and Public Administration. Zoology was my graduation subject but Public Administration was new to me, so I had to carefully read the relevant textbooks multiple times while covering the syllabus. On the night before the Public Administration mains paper, I was nervous. *Ima* knew it was an important exam for me, and with her motherly instinct, advised me to sleep so that I would be well-rested for the next day. I couldn't sleep, so I continued studying. *Ima* woke up at intervals and urged me to stop reading and get up early instead. When the lights went out, she lit a candle and told me to wrap up my studies. I said, "Yes, *Ima*," but I continued reading until past midnight, until dawn. As usual, *Dada* dropped me at the examination hall, and I managed to write the paper.

Finally, my main papers were over. When the results were announced, I was relieved to see my name on the noticeboard alongside other successful candidates—I had cleared the mains examinations! The final hurdle was the viva voce. As the schedules for the viva voce were released, I found myself anxiously immersed in my books and newspapers once more, practising how to respond to questions orally.

Before the final results of the Manipur Public Service Commission competitive exam were announced, our usual bedtime conversations revolved around the likelihood of my selection. *Ima* would reassure me, saying that if there were no corruption or unfair practices, I stood a good chance. Our only hope was that I would be selected based on merit. Though nervous, I wasn't overly anxious. I had already been selected as an SSA primary teacher and was on the verge of joining my school. I had made up my mind to start working and to continue taking competitive examinations until I succeeded.

Then, the fateful day arrived, and I received the news that the results had been published. I couldn't believe my eyes when I saw my name among the selected candidates—I had achieved my dream and was about to join the Manipur Civil Service! Our entire family was overjoyed. *Ima* and I were so excited that we couldn't sleep that night. We spent the time smiling and laughing in disbelief. We were both speechless—it was one of the happiest moments we had ever shared. It was because of her sheer belief in me, her perseverance and unwavering support throughout my life, that my studies bore fruit and shaped my career. It was a victory for her dreams, for all the sacrifices she had made for us, and together we thanked God, as always.

For *Ima*, it was another victory—her dedication to ensuring our strength, independence, and success had helped us to achieve these goals. At the felicitation ceremony where we were honoured, *Ima* held her head high. While I was thrilled to express gratitude for the congratulations, my heart swelled with happiness when *Ima* came to the stage to address the audience gathered in the hall. I couldn't hold back my tears. I don't recall her exact words, but I felt the joy, pride, and happiness she expressed. It was a moment when we felt that our long journey of effort, perseverance, patience, and hard work had paid off.

Yet, one concern continued to bother *Ima*—my marriage. As a mother, she felt a strong sense of responsibility to arrange my marriage, viewing it as her final duty. In 2015, I married Yaiphaba Longjam, who also serves in the Manipur Civil Service. Although we were acquaintances from our Vision IAS coaching days, our friendship deepened after we both joined the service, eventually leading to marriage.

As my wedding day drew near, I realised my life was about to change. Being *Ima*'s youngest child, the thought of leaving her weighed heavily on my heart. *Ima* felt the same way but hid her sadness, determined to fulfil her role as a mother. I felt a pang of sorrow, knowing that a physical distance would soon separate us. Everything was about to change: mornings would no longer start with her waking me up, and our closeness would have to be forsaken. The separation between a daughter and her mother is never simple, but as always, *Ima* faced this reality with courage and supported me, ensuring I stayed strong. She wore a smile to convey her excitement and happiness for my marriage, even as she masked her own emotions.

In Meitei tradition, during a daughter's marriage, the mother remains at home (that is, the bride's residence), and does not participate in the wedding procession to the groom's place after the marriage ceremony. The next day, the bride's mother can visit her daughter at the groom's residence. When my sisters got married, a relative always stayed behind to keep *Ima* company at home. Each time her daughters married, she would cry her heart out, grappling with the separation. Our brothers' marriages were livelier as we welcomed new additions to our family.

Ima was deeply involved in every aspect of my marriage, ensuring nothing was overlooked in the preparations. On the day of my wedding, after the marriage ceremony concluded at our home and the moment came to step out, I felt a heavy weight in my heart. People advised me not to cry, warning that my tears would bring sorrow to my maternal home—a saying that seemed insensitive, and traditions and customs that felt so harsh. Even though I tried hard to remain composed, tears flowed freely when *Ima* blessed me by stroking my head. When my brothers wished me a happy married life, I couldn't hold back my emotions.

According to Meitei custom, I entered the bridal car alone because *Ima* could not accompany me in the wedding procession to the groom's place. She hid her tears and bid me farewell with a faint smile. The heavy burden she had carried since *Baba* left, leaving her alone with the responsibilities of us six, finally lifted that day.

The day after the wedding, *Ima* came to my new home in Keishamthong, Imphal West, to shower me with her blessings before bidding farewell. She smiled, but I could sense that she was concealing her pain—a pain that had been inevitable since the day she gave birth to a daughter, knowing that one day her daughter would leave home to live with her spouse. With courage, she accepted this destined sorrow, just as she had done for her other daughters.

11

Farewell

Ima started facing serious health issues around 2013. She was diagnosed with a weak heart and received long-term medication after a cardiologist's examination. In her 30s and 40s, she struggled with neuromuscular issues that resulted in numbness and indescribable pain. *Baba* consulted many doctors, but the treatments gave only temporary relief. Over time, the weakness in her nerves remained, and she developed severe knee pain. In addition, she also contracted *Herpes zoster* (shingles) on her shoulder around 2014, further weakening her nerves. After recovering from the infection, she began attending yoga classes. Initially, she attended classes outside, but later began practising at home, incorporating yoga into her daily routine. She did yoga every morning and evening, which helped alleviate her pain. Although she could no longer walk long distances as easily as before, she continued to go for morning walks whenever she felt better.

It seemed that all the physical work she had tirelessly done in the past was now taking a heavy toll on her health. She constantly felt weak, and because she couldn't describe the pain caused by her nerves, doctors struggled to alleviate it. They explained that she was experiencing bone weakening due to ageing. For the pain in her knees, doctors suggested physiotherapy. She underwent sessions, but the pain persisted. Injections in her knees provided temporary relief, but the knee pain became a constant companion she could not shake off. She often sweated profusely and felt exhausted, needing to rest at home frequently and sometimes skipping visits to *Ima Keithel.* However, whenever she felt slightly better, she would rise from her bed and then go to sell her shawls. Going to *Ima Keithel* provided a kind of solace for her.

In 2017, *Ima* fell seriously ill and was diagnosed with diabetes. She remained bedridden for about a month, but gradually her health began to improve. She recovered, and we all took precautions to ensure she followed the correct diet. *Ima* disliked the sugarless food and *champhut*—the tasteless steamed and boiled vegetables she had to eat. She particularly missed rice, making it hard for her to reduce her intake. Almost everything she enjoyed eating was considerably reduced from her diet. She carried sugar-free sweetener tablets for her tea at home and even at *Ima Keithel.* Although she regained her health, we all noticed she had become weak. Keen to recover, *Ima* continued her exercises and yoga. She accompanied *Dada* for routine check-ups with her cardiologist and continued her medications and physiotherapy.

In 2018, we thought of skipping *Ningol Chakkouba* because *Ima* had just recovered from illness and needed rest. However, she insisted that we celebrate it. *Ningol Chakkouba* has always been a cherished occasion for our family to gather, so we all joyfully assembled at her home. My sister-in-law Anita had prepared delicious dishes for the special day but had gone to her maternal home with my niece Angelina and nephew Zoshuan for the *Ningol Chakkouba* luncheon. *Damcha* was stationed at Chakrata with his family and could not join. Present at the luncheon were *Dada,* the four sisters, and our children, and we all enjoyed our family time together.

After the luncheon, we got *dakhinas* (gifts) from *Ima* and *Dada* along with their blessings. My nieces Priyadarshini and Stacia, nephews Priyobrata, Melvin, Parambir, and Harris, and my son Machanghen played boisterously together. They received their *dakhina*s with much excitement and grinning faces. *Ima* delighted in watching them and how they bestowed blessings upon her, mimicking the words elders usually say, "*Nungaina pallu sangna punshiyu*!" (May you be blessed with a blissful and long life).

Days passed in their usual routine. *Dada* continued taking *Ima* for regular check-ups. Meanwhile, I was expecting my second baby (Yailen). *Ima* came to meet me at my home, and following the Meitei tradition, brought items like pots, rice, and smoked fish during my last month of pregnancy. Together with my in-laws, we shared a meal. As my delivery date approached, I went shopping with my sister Dhanabati to *Ima Keithel* to buy essential items for the baby. We visited *Ima's potpham* to meet her. She was wearing a light pink shawl and, as usual, greeted us with her customary warm smile. She advised me to buy extra *ningdhas* (plain cotton cloths for wrapping newborns). We bought these from *Laxmi Keithel*, just a few stalls away from her *potpham*. She invited me for lunch and asked what I wanted to eat. As per Meitei tradition, a pregnant daughter is invited for lunch at her maternal home during the final month of pregnancy.

On 25 December 2018, I went to my maternal home for lunch. *Ima* was waiting eagerly for my arrival with my son on the front porch, dressed in a saffron-coloured *phanek* and sweater. We enjoyed a hearty meal together with *Ima*, my sister-in-law, and niece. After lunch, we chatted in our usual way. *Iche* Memma, *Ima's* niece Indira, who was married and lived nearby, also joined us. My son was running around, but *Ima* found it hard to chase him due to her painful knee. Nevertheless, she played with him. In the evening, when I bid goodbye, she smiled and waved as our car departed. Little did I know it would be the last time I would see her.

All six of us had settled into our own lives, and like most families, we were caught up in our daily routines of household chores and careers. Though we kept in touch with *Ima* over the phone, the physical distance remained. Whenever she longed to see all, she did not wait for us to visit her; she would come to us instead. My sister Dhanabati had invited *Ima* for lunch at her home, and *Ima* was delighted with the *ngahei* (fish) Dhanabati specially prepared for her. Shortly after, *Ima* also visited Kemila and Promila at their homes to spend time with them and their families. She even went to see her elder sister Sakhi. Little did we know, she was bidding farewell to everyone.

On 1 January 2019, when I called *Ima* in the evening, she mentioned she had done her usual exercises and yoga. She had also gone for her routine check-up with *Dada* to her cardiologist, who informed her that she was improving and reduced some of her daily medications. She shared that she had visited Promila's house that afternoon. During our conversation, *Ima* also spoke to my son, Machanghen, on the phone, asking him if he wanted sweets. I sought her advice on what to pack for my delivery and what items needed to be bought in advance. She suggested that, since it was winter, extra blankets would be needed for the relatives staying with me overnight at the hospital. Our conversation ended that evening—and forever.

On the early morning of 4 January 2019, around 6.30 a.m., I received a distressing call from my niece Angelina and sister Promila informing me that *Ima* had suffered a cardiac arrest. They urged me rush to RIMS Hospital immediately. Filled with dread and foreboding, I hurried to the casualty. There, I found *Ima* lying on the bed with her eyes closed, appearing deeply asleep. Her hands were cold when I touched them. Despite our efforts to wake her by calling her name and rubbing her hands to warm her, she remained unresponsive. I recalled her saying, "A day will come when I will not answer," whenever she was very angry. These words now echoed in my mind, conveying her extreme anger, though we knew she did not mean what she said. She lay peacefully as if sleeping, free from all pain and illness. She had departed, letting go of everything in her life. But when *Ima* left us, she did so only after fulfilling all her commitments and promises to us.

Epilogue

The sudden demise of *Ima* left us grief-stricken. We felt bereft, thinking of the countless conversations we wished we could have had, the gestures we wanted to make for her, and the precious moments we hoped to share with her. *Ima* devoted everything to us—her life, love, hopes, and dreams. Her departure brought sadness not only to our family but also to our relatives, acquaintances, and her friends in *Ima Keithel.* She left behind a void that could never be filled.

Ima's life was not an easy one, yet her journey is worth remembering for the courage and conviction with which she faced life. With sheer willpower, she changed the tides of her life and emerged as a survivor, a true winner. When our father left her alone with six of us, our future hung in uncertainty. *Ima* had to accept widowhood and embrace her circumstances. We owe our lives and achievements to our parents, especially our beloved *Ima,* who bestowed upon us love, support, invaluable life lessons, a solid education, and the drive to become capable individuals. We grew up into independent, self-reliant people, just as they wished us to be.

It is easy for anyone to succumb to life's challenges—criticisms, illnesses, or tough times. However, *Ima* stood her ground because she knew what truth was. She faced sicknesses, financial burdens, frustrations, fatigue, depression, the daily pressures of work, and the uncertainties of loss and gain. She also took on the responsibility of addressing our aspirations, demands, resolving arguments, managing family disputes, and navigating the competitive world.

Ima was a righteous person who fulfilled her duties diligently to God, her family, and society. She forgave those who wronged her and adhered strictly to ethics and values. It is said that children learn by observing their parents, and that is exactly what we did. Her constant guidance, practical advice, emotional support, and decisive moments taught us how to handle every situation. Through her wisdom, she equipped us with the mental strength needed to overcome difficulties, while her love brought joy and peace into our lives.

Whether it was our education, personal struggles, careers, relationships, or starting our own families, *Ima* always imparted the golden advice: to stay steadfast, determined, and do the right thing. Her counsel has always guided us in every sphere of our lives. With a prayer in her heart, she faced life boldly. She wished us happiness in our marriages and success in our careers. She treated everyone with equal respect and honour, inspiring us and many other people who knew her with her hard work, integrity, and compassion for humanity.

Ima is dearly missed and fondly remembered by her family and the extended family of *Ima Keithel.*

Ima's story depicts facets of the life of a Manipuri woman and her umbilical connection to *Ima Keithel.* Her narrative holds great significance as it highlights the common struggle faced by thousands of Manipuri weavers, underscores the importance of

Manipuri handlooms, and illuminates the unique journeys of the women vendors of *Ima Keithel.* These women not only earn their livelihood and provide for their families but also emerge as strong, independent individuals. Each of them has a special experience and story that often goes untold.

The skilled craftsmanship and weaving techniques of Manipuri women not only give them an occupation and identity but also contribute to the cultural richness of our land. Manipuri handlooms stand as a proud cultural heritage of the state, upheld by dedicated weavers who preserve this beautiful tradition. The legacy of Manipuri handlooms, Manipuri women, and their association with *Ima Keithel* will continue to be cherished for generations to come.

It's not just Manipuri weavers; all Manipuri women play a crucial role in sustaining their families and contributing to society. Their contributions are vital to the economic development of Manipur, spanning various sectors such as agriculture, fisheries, the handloom industry, small-scale food industries, the paper industry, pottery, handicrafts, salt production, doll making, and more. Whether as daily wage earners, domestic helpers, labourers, farmers, artisans, or small-scale entrepreneurs, they selflessly work for the betterment of their families, thereby strengthening the social fabric of Manipur.

These women also serve as torchbearers of Manipuri society, as evidenced by their pivotal roles in the *Nupilan*s (Women's Wars) of 1904 and 1939, where they courageously protested oppressive administrative policies during the British colonial rule. The daily struggles faced by many widows in Manipur, like *Ima*, who are the sole breadwinners for their families, involve meeting family expenses, educating their children, managing healthcare and marriage expenses, and fulfilling civic duties. And this struggle is both beautiful and worthwhile.

To sum up, *Weaving Dreams – Ima's Memoir of Empowerment: A Life Entwined with Manipur's Rich Legacy* tells the story of a Manipuri woman who believed in self-respect and self-worth. It is a tale of resilience and grit. Despite being born into a poor family, her hard work empowered her to become self-reliant and find purpose in her daily life. The memoir also chronicles her journey to *Ima Keithel*, which is Asia's largest all-women market, highlighting its historical significance and continued importance today.

In contemporary times, we often find ourselves captivated by tales of success, power, and fame, but these are not the only aspirations. Being a survivor, living with dignity, maintaining self-worth and high self-esteem, appreciating the value of hard work and discipline, embracing entrepreneurship, and having the courage to confront life's unpredictable challenges—these are the hallmarks of a fulfilling life. This memoir, penned by a daughter to fulfil her promise to her mother, aims to convey the reality of daily struggles we all face. It is my earnest hope that this memoir will inspire you, dear reader, to live purposeful life filled with courage.

Let me conclude this memoir with a poem I wrote for my mother, dedicated to her.

An Angel Divine

I have known an Angel divine,
I have known love divine.

An Angel, she worked day and night;
An Angel, she sweated for us.

Ever aware of our needs and wants,
Ever aware of our well-being.

Showering her prayers to the Lord,
Showering all blessings unto us.

Hiding a tear, hiding a cry,
Hiding fears, bearing all hardships.

Against all intimidations,
Against all injustices.

Caring with her unwavering love,
Ever trying to correct us when we went astray.

With a faith firm, she stood by truth,
With courage she crossed obstacles mighty and many.

Ima, our dearest and beloved Mother,
You are an Angel divine!

You are an eternal soul,
A true devotee of Him.

A hearty smile always on your face,
A healthy life was all we wished for you.

Forgive us, dear Mother,
Forgive us for our misdeeds and hurt we caused.

In your footsteps, we will walk,
In your belief that work is life.

The bravest, the most courageous of all;
Ima, you are the Divine Angel in our life.

Glossary

Arangpham: A professional person who assists in arranging all rituals for religious/cultural/traditional ceremonies in Meitei society

Athenpot: *An* offering of vegetables, fruits, and other items, to a deity

Awunpot: Gifts by maternal parents to a bride in her trousseau in the Meitei tradition

Barti: A type of incense stick

Bobok: Grandmother

Chakchafida: A small rectangular mat to sit on while having a meal

Chakkouba: Luncheon

Charik: Necklace

Chengfu: A traditional pot for storing rice used by Meiteis

Chengjen wanba: A term used for buying rice

Ching: Hill

Heddle: A set of parallel cords/rods through which each thread in the warp passes to separate the warp threads.

Iche: Elder sister

Inama: Sister-in-law

Inaphee: Lady's stole

Innjao: Fishing net

Kabok aphaba: Puffed rice

Keinasennabi: A lady who stays with a bride throughout the Meitei wedding ceremony and helps her through all the rituals

Khoimayek: The circular pattern that resembles a fish hook in the border of a *mapannaibi phanek*

Khudei: Meitei traditional attire for males

Khudeng: Traditional small bathtub used by Meiteis

Khujai: A small utensil used for drinking water

Kokyet: A Meitei white *pagri* (headdress)

Kon: Manipuri fly shuttle loom, consisting of a wooden frame for weaving that is equipped with wooden devices

Kouna: *Schoenoplectus sp.*, a plant used to make various mats and handicrafts

Kuthi eeba panji: Birth chart or horoscope readers

Leikai: Locality

Leima Jagoi: A dance form of the Meitei community

Leirak: Street

Leisabi: Unmarried girl

Lengyan: A traditional Manipuri stole

Longhup: A fish trap made of bamboo

Long: A spear-like bamboo pole with its top consisting of pointed bamboo fingers to catch fish

Luhong phan: A groom's wedding seat

Mandap: A temporary venue where a wedding ceremony is solemnised

Mangol: Front porch

Marup: A type of saving scheme where a monthly contribution is collected from all members at a fixed rate and given by turn to a member every month. The scheme ends when all members get their share of the contribution

Mayek: Motif

Meiphoo: A portable iron charcoal burner

Meitei pung: A Meitei barrel-shaped percussion musical instrument

Meiteilon: The Manipuri language

Nahong: A baby sling

Ngari: Fermented fish

Nga ayaiba: A smoked fish

Ngarubak: A traditional bamboo basket used to store fish

Ningdha: Plain cotton clothes used to wrap newborn babies

Ningol: Daughter

Nupi: Woman

Oja: A teacher

Ongbi: A Manipuri word used to denote that a woman has been married and has joined a new family. It is placed between her spouse's family surname and her maiden name; for example, Oinam *Ongbi* Memcha

Paiya: Bamboo threads

Pakhan: A small lodging in front of a house

Phambal: A throne

Phanek: A traditional wraparound skirt worn by Meitei women

Phee: Cloth

Pheematek: A stole worn by Manipuri women

Pheesashang: A weaving shed

Pheijom: Traditional attire for Meitei men

Polang: A woven bamboo basket

Potpham: A market stall

Pukham: A brass/steel plate used for serving rice

Pukhri: A pond

Pumngou phanek: A pale pink traditional sarong worn by Meitei women for death ceremonies or for prayer ceremonies at home, temples, or any other venue

Pungyat: Upper body dress worn by men of the Meitei community

Pung chollom: A unique classical dance form of Manipur

Samtu pheematek: Woollen shawls

Sanaboon: Traditional water-storing utensil of the Meiteis

Sanamahism: The indigenous religion of the Meiteis

Shamuk: A brass stand

Shraddha: Rituals observed for offering prayers to a deceased member of a family

Shumang Leelas: Manipuri outdoor theatre dramas

Shuttle: A spindle-shaped tool that carries the spool of the weft yarn

Spool: A small cylindrical piece of wood on which yarn is wound by spinning, for use in weaving

Soibum: Fermented bamboo shoots

Tareng: Wooden spinning wheel

Thaomei podhon: A lamp with a thread in a tin can, lit with kerosene

Thumok: Traditional hand-woven bamboo basket

Tirth mapan: A pilgrimage to worship at nine religious' sites

Tonga: Horse-drawn carriage

Treadle: Foot pedals of a loom

U-mangra: Tapioca root

Uppu kangdhon: Furniture, such as beds, cupboards, tables, and chairs

Ushop: Luncheon

Uyungs: Thin wooden poles

Wari: Story

Warp: A set of yarns/thread stretched on a loom

Yangkok: A circular cane basket for winnowing rice chaff

Yongchak: *Parkia speciosa*, a plant on which bitter beans grow

Yumjao: A Meitei traditional house

Yumsharol: A treatise on the fundamental principles of the construction of a traditional Meitei house

References

Cheitharol Kumbaba (The royal court chronicle of the kings of Manipur), Translation work, Imphal: Manipur State Archives, pp.1–1105.

Dun, E.W. 1975. *Gazetteer of Manipur.* Delhi: Vivek Publishing House, reprint, p.64.

Evolutionary Growth of the Khwairamband Keithel, Imphal: Manipur Research Society, 2003, pp.1–18.

Grimwood, Ethel St. Clair. 1891. My Three Years in Manipur. London: Richard Bentley and Sons, and New Delhi: Gain Publishing House, reprint, 2000, p.43.

Hodson, T.C. 2009. *The Meitheis* (1908). Delhi: Low Price Publications, reprint, p.23.

Manipur: Panorama of Handlooms and Handicrafts, Mission for Economic Empowerment of Traditional Artisans and Craftsmen (MEETAC), National Institute of Design, 2020, pp. 39–163.

Shaya Devi, T. 2009. *Traditional Tribal Dresses of Manipur (Museum Collections).* Manipur State Museum, Bulletin, (November) Vol. III, pp. 59–68.

Author's *Baba* Daoji Oinam and *Ima* Oinam Ongbi Memcha

Ima before her marriage

Ima with her childhood friend Sobita

Ima with her eldest daughter Kemila

(Top row, L-R): Robert, Kemila, Dhanabati and cousin sister Bijaya. (Middle row): Cousin brothers Solomon and Daniel. (Bottom row): *Ima*, with the author in her lap, along with Promila and Tiken

Baba at Sekmai Police Station, Manipur, in 1992, where he was stationed

Baba and *Ima* with their children. Standing (L-R): Robert, Kemila, author, Dhanabati, and Tiken. Promila is seated next to *Baba.* Seen in the background is the author's family house under construction

Ima and her *kon* (circled in blue) in the Mangol

A Manipuri *kon*

Ima placing the insignias on Tiken after the Passing out Parade (POP) at the Officers Training Academy (OTA) in Chennai, on 22 September 2007

An aerial view of the three *Ima* Markets

Three Ima Keithels (popularly known as Ima Market) in one frame

Emoinu Ima Keithel (previously known as Laxmi *Keithel*)

Rows and sections in *Ima Keithel*

Ima at her *potpham* (stall)

Different varieties of Manipuri shawls and stoles sold by *Ima* at *Ima Keithel*

(The nomenclature of these shawls is based on the terminology used by women vendors in *Ima Keithel* and does not correspond to the actual names used by different communities in their respective dialects)

Salai taret shawl (also known as rainbow shawl)

Chaka shawl

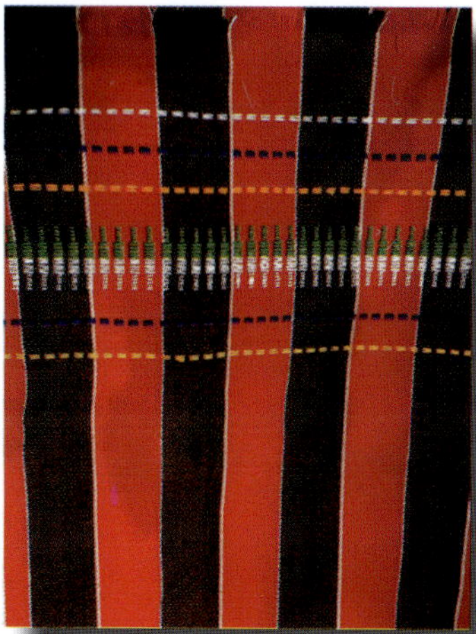

Chungkham Araiba shawl

Houra Araiba shawl

Tongkap shawl

A 2-ply yarn *Pheejao*

Leiroom shawl

Tangkhul shawl

Naga shawl

Kuki shawl

Nupi phee 2-ply *Arangba*

Nupi phee 2-ply yarn *Arangba*

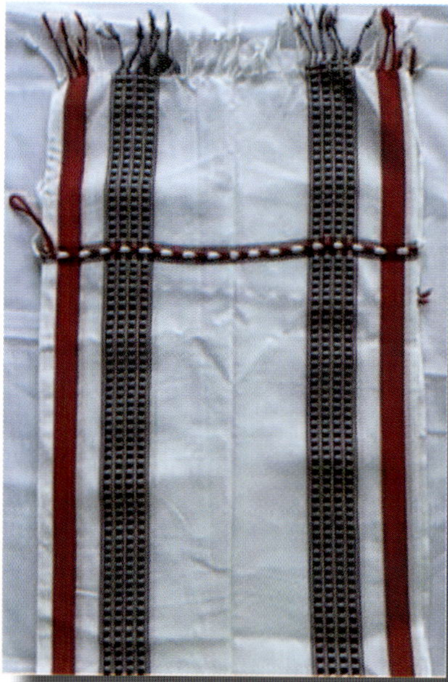

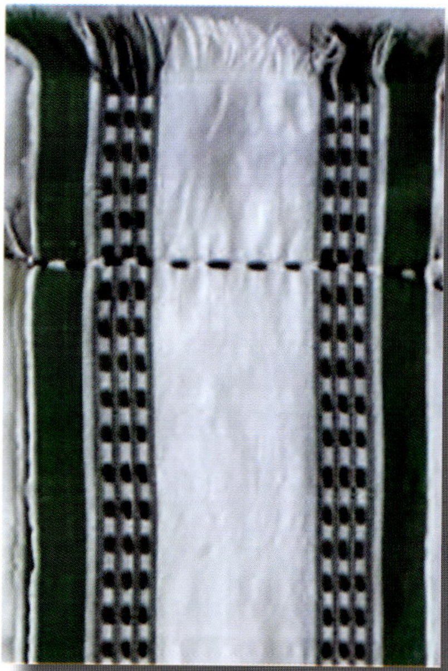

Leiroom lengyan *Leiroom lengyan*

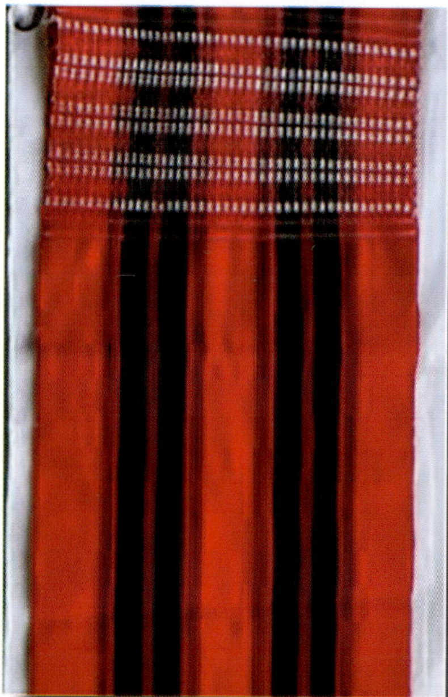

Lengyan *Chaka Ataibi* shawl

Index

4th National Handloom Census Reports (2019-20) 79

Achou, Oinam, Uncle 17–18, 58
Adversity xiv, 63
All India Handloom Census for 2019–20 11
Anuradha Usham xvii
Artisans 2, 146
Arts 13, 99
Athenpot 63, 117
Awamphi 12
Awunpot 10, 73, 94

Baazi 2–4
Baba 7–8, 17–22, 24–27, 31–33, 40, 43–44, 46–52, 54, 56–60, 62–71, 91–92, 96, 104–05, 108, 115–17, 137, 139
  accident 65, 66, 67
  as an assistant sub-inspector (ASI) in the Manipur Police Department 8, 17
  as a police inspector and officer-in-charge 49
  a self-made man 18
  commitment to duty 46
  death xv, 67, 69–70, 92, 104–05, 108
  duties and responsibilities 49
  Ima's devoted care 66
  paralyzed 66
  promotion to the rank of Deputy Superintendent of Police (DSP) 66
  strict rules 57
Bamboo baskets 27–28, 45, 79, 115
Bamboo products 80
Bamon Mema 87
Bedsheet(s) 10, 14, 32, 35, 87
Belief and faith xiii–iv, 5, 17–18, 89, 91, 100, 104–05, 136, 148
Bino, sister 3, 34
Birth charts 19, 58, 105
Blankets 10, 79, 142

Candles 26, 62, 78, 111
  making 80
Central Silk Board of India 7
Ceremony(ies) 11, 24, 26, 68, 92–96, 121, 136–37
Chabon (boiled rice water) 25, 27
Chakkouba or ushop 26, 92–93, 96
  mapam 92–93, 96
Chakrata 122–23, 141
Cheitharol Kumbaba 13, 30, 77
Chemcha 48, 53
Chengfu (a traditional rice pot for storing rice) 31, 35, 45, 62
Chengjen wanba 4
Childhood 8, 29, 48, 55, 102, 119

Cloth/Clothing 4, 9, 12, 14, 25, 27, 32, 35–38, 42, 49, 54, 64, 69, 80–82, 84, 87, 109, 114, 131, 141
handloom 14
thickness and appearance 36
traditional 114
types of 42
woven 14
Combined Defence Services (CDS) 101
Short Service Commission 101
Compassion 46, 145
Competitive examinations 60, 97–98, 100, 131, 135
Confidence 6, 59, 84, 120, 128
Cooking 3, 18, 26–27, 45, 52, 55, 81, 121
Courage xiv, xvii, 1, 48, 78, 91, 126, 137–38, 144, 147–48
Craftsmanship 10, 146
Credit and borrowing 31–33, 38
Cultural
heritage 10, 11, 146
richness 146
Culture 29, 92, 112
Customers 73–75, 79, 87–89, 103
budget-conscious 74
Hindi-speaking 103
satisfaction 89
Customs 10, 18, 92, 133–34, 137
traditional 92

Damcha, Tiken, brother 48, 50–51, 53, 96–98, 101–02, 118–19, 121–23, 129, 141
Dance(s) 44, 56, 94, 127–28
Dancing 2, 56, 127
Daoji Oinam, father 17
David, Oinam 56, 118
Dedication xiv–xv, 41–42, 91–92, 100, 120, 136
Deity(ies) 5, 26, 29–30, 63–64, 87, 89, 105–06, 112–13
local 64, 105, 112
Meitei 105
pre-Hindu 113
Designs and patterns 1–2, 9–14, 54, 72–75, 79, 85–87
floral and animal 12, 72
flower 14
indigenous and vibrant weft- woven 11
local 12
lui (a diagonal weft pattern) 73
Moirang pheejin 86
pungri haophee 74
rhombus 13
spear 74
triangular 11
weft-woven 11
Determination xiv, xvii, 16–17, 42, 75, 79, 121, 133
Devotion xv, 111–12, 117
Dhanabati, sister xvi, 27, 48, 66, 69, 96–98, 100, 141–42
joined the Manipur Police as a constable 100
teaching at a private school 69, 96, 100
Dignity xv, 15, 147
Discipline xiv, 46, 55, 58, 61, 120, 147
military 120
Divine xiv, 147–48
Drama(s) 56, 108–09

Earnings 4, 7, 14, 34–35, 59, 75, 80
Economic
activity 83
development 146
empowerment xv, 78
Economy 76, 78
Education xvi, 4, 7–8, 59, 61, 69, 81, 133, 144–45
college 133
formal 61
higher 7
school 133
transformative power of xvi
Ekashini, Ima's eldest sister 3, 5–6, 22
abducted 6
Embroidery 4, 8, 13–15

Emoinu Ima Keithel (Laxmi Ima Keithel) 40, 86, 90, 131, 141
Emotional support xiii, 145
Employment 5, 69, 80
Entrepreneurial spirit xvii, 80
Entrepreneurship 79, 147

Fabric(s) 10–12, 14, 35, 80, 95
Family(ies)
  breakup of 15
  disintegration of 15
  expenses 4, 14, 31, 71, 81, 146
  extended 90, 145
  finances 58, 76, 80
  financial stability 41
  income 35
  joint 18
  maternal 73, 114
  needs of 23, 58, 92
  pension 69
  poor xiv, 4, 15–16, 147
  reunion 110
  source of income for 32
Festival(s) 62, 74, 105–06, 114, 116–17
  annual 105
  Meitei New Year 106
  Rath Yatra 117
Films/Movie(s) 2–3, 52, 108–09, 123
  Bollywood 52, 123
  Hindi 28
  Manipuri 2
Financial
  balance 41
  burden 31, 96, 145
  challenges 78
  constraints 4, 64, 69
  crises 78
  crunch 40
  independence 42, 80
  problems 41, 132
Friendship 6–7, 37, 42, 88, 102–03, 126–27, 130, 136

Girls 22, 26, 32, 56, 95, 129
  unmarried 32, 95

Gokul, Oinam, Uncle 17–18, 58, 115
Government of Manipur 58, 83–85, 89, 96, 100
Guru Atiya Sidaba, the Supreme Eternal Godhead 29

Handicrafts 76, 78–79, 86, 123–24, 146
  products 79, 81
Handloom xv, 1–2, 4, 10–14, 32–33, 71–72, 76, 78–81, 86–87, 146
  clusters 11
  production 11
Handloom products 1, 11–12, 14, 32, 71, 76, 79–80
  haophees 71, 74
  kukiphees 71
  leiroomphees 71, 73, 88
  linmayeks 72
  luiphees 71, 73, 88
  manggamphees 71
  nupiphees 71
  pheemateks 72, 86
  tindongbi 72
  woollen 71
Handloom weaving xiv–xv, 4, 7, 10–15, 21, 28, 32–33, 35–37, 39–42, 55, 59, 72, 78, 80, 146–47
  abilities 41
  as a symbol of status for women 13
  cloth 12
  community xv
  methods of 12
  network xiv, 33
  process 36
  silk 13
  textile 12
  traditional 10–11
Hardship(s) xiii–xv, 7, 23, 30, 32, 42, 48, 66, 68, 70, 75, 89, 91, 130, 132, 148
  economic 89
  financial 32, 42
  physical xiii
Hiyangthang Lairembi, Goddess 114
Household(s) 11, 17–19, 22–25, 27–30, 37, 43, 52–53, 59, 68–69, 76, 79–80,

economy 76
entrepreneurs of 90
hill districts of 12
insurgency movements 56
law and order situation in 57
merged with the Indian Union on 15 October 1949 57
President's rule 83
weavers of 1
weaving skills in 10
Manipur Civil Services Examination 109, 134
Manipur Development Society (MDS) 83, 85
Manipuri handlooms 11–12, 32, 79, 146
Manipuri loom xv, 4, 7, 10, 12–13, 27, 35–37, 40, 73, 79, 80
backstrap 12
body-tension 12
fly shuttle 35
loin 12
products 13
shuttle 12
types of 12
Manipuri society 4, 70, 80, 92, 145–46
Manipuri weaver(s) xiii, xv, 37–38, 41, 80, 145–46
local 59, 72
network of xv, 41–42, 72
skilled 34, 37, 39, 72
supportive network of xv
talented 1, 34
woollen shawl 72
Manipuri women xiii, xv–xvi, 1, 6, 9–11, 13, 22–23, 28, 32, 34, 38, 42, 44, 54, 72–87, 95–96, 109, 114, 120–21, 133, 145–47
decision-making autonomy 81
economic empowerment xv
elderly 81
engage in economic activities 81
hardworking and courageous 82
industrious and entrepreneurial spirit 80
married 32, 81, 114, 133
Meitei 22
rural 80
survival and sustenance of 76
tribal 109
unmarried 81
Manipur Public Service Commission 135
Manipur Research Society, Imphal 76
Manipur University 96, 100, 102, 131–32
Marketing 78, 83–84
Marriage/Wedding 2, 5–8, 14–15, 18–19, 26, 73–74, 88, 92–96, 99–100, 136–38, 145, 147
Marups 35, 41
monthly 41
tender 35
Maslai mateks 7, 13
Mayang Imphal 20–21, 43
Meitei(s) 3, 5, 8–13, 17, 19, 22, 26–27, 29–30, 40, 44–45, 56, 62–63, 68, 76–77, 88, 92–95, 104–06, 113, 115, 117, 121, 127, 133, 137, 141
indigenous religion of the 5
Vaishnavite 106
Meitei Yumsharol 19
Mema, Iche 87
Memcha 1, 34, 87
Memcha, Bobok 109
Memtombi, Iche 37
Memtombi, Yaikhom 24, 34
Moirang 7–9, 11, 14, 47–48, 72, 79, 86–87, 111, 113–14
Moneylenders 31, 34, 99
Moreh 39, 43
Mosquito nets 28, 32–35, 37–40, 42, 59, 73, 86–87
Mota, Ekashini's daughter 22
Motherhood xvii, 22–23, 30, 100
Motifs 1, 7, 9–12, 14, 72, 74, 87, 95
designs of 14
flower 72, 87
likli (bottle) 12, 74
Moirang pheejin 7–9, 11, 14, 86–87

snake 72
spear 74
Mufflers 10, 28, 86
Music 95, 107–08
Myth/Mythology 9, 11, 13, 30, 77, 113

National Cadet Corps (NCC) 96–97, 101, 118, 128–30
activities 97, 129
National Handloom Census Report, 2010 11
National Handloom Development Programme 11
Ngarubak 35, 45
Nilapadma Higher Secondary School 52
Ningol Chakkouba 32, 62, 74, 114–16, 140–41
Nolini, Ekashini's daughter 22
Nungshi, Soyam 34
Nupa Pala 2, 94–95
Nupi Keithel 75
Nupilans (Women's Wars) 146

Officers Training Academy (OTA), Chennai 118–21
Oinam, Angelina, Ima's first grandchild 99–100, 110, 122–23, 141, 143
Oinams xvii, 17–19, 56, 58, 100, 120–21

Panthoibi, goddess 13
Paona Bazaar 83, 86
Paonam Ongbi Tolen, father's eldest sister 7–8, 17, 21, 47, 115
Parashmani, R.K. 100
Passing Out Parade (POP) 118–21
Passion 15, 72, 79
Patience 3, 48, 136
Phanek(s) 8–10, 12, 15, 32, 35, 42, 49, 72, 86–87, 95, 111–15, 121, 142
mapannaibi 49, 95, 115, 121
mayek naibi 15
mayeknaibi 86
pumngou 111
Phee(s) 9, 11–12, 14, 32, 42, 73, 79, 87, 94–95, 121
cotton 12
Khurkhul muga 12
mateks 32, 42
maslai 12
Moirang 9, 11, 79
Rani 79, 87, 95, 121
Wangkhei 12, 79, 87, 95
woollen 73
Pheijom matups 13
Pheingao pheisois 13
Phouoibee Ima Keithel 86
Pishum Leima 76
Pocket money 39, 41, 69
Postpartum dietary practices 22
Potpham (stall), Ima Keithel 1, 40, 71–73, 78, 85–88, 90, 131, 141
Poverty xvi, 15
Prayers 26, 28, 54, 62–63, 73, 89, 93–94, 105–06, 111–13, 117, 148
daily 105
Profits and savings 7, 13–14, 19, 33–34, 40–41, 66, 74, 88–89, 92, 99
Promila Oinam, Dr, sister xvi, xvii, 27, 47–48, 52, 65–66, 69, 96, 100, 104, 115, 142–43
dedication and hard work 100
earned her Master's and doctoral degree (PhD) 100, 104
selected as an assistant professor in the Education Department 100
Prosperity 5, 32, 93, 113
Public Works Department (PWD) 83, 85

Ramkumar, brother 2–3, 5
Ranjit Battalion 120
Raw material(s) 80
Regional Institute of Medical Sciences (RIMS), Imphal 98, 143
Regional Tasar Research Station 7
Religion 5, 29, 30, 63, 112
Religious
products 79
site(s) 111–14

Resilience xiv, 121, 147
Rice 3–5, 18, 22, 25–28, 31, 35, 45, 55, 59, 63–64, 67, 76, 87, 89–90, 93, 106, 117–18, 121, 140–41
  husking 3, 18
  puffed 5, 25, 87, 93
  storage of 45
Rite(s)/Ritual(s) 2, 11, 26, 62, 68, 87, 93–95, 105, 112, 117
Robert (Dada) xvi, 23, 48, 52, 66, 68–69, 92–94, 96, 99, 135, 140–42
  as an arts graduate teacher 99
  Bachelor's in Education (BEd) 99
  teaching job at a private school 92, 99

Sajibu Cheiraoba or Sajibu Nongma Panba 62–65, 106
Sakhi, sister 3–5, 32, 142
Sales 2, 14, 33, 40, 71, 73–75, 84, 87–90, 103, 132
  daily 40, 71, 75, 90
Samtu phee mateks (woollen shawls) 32
Sanamahi 29–30
Sanamahism 5, 26, 29, 63, 68, 87, 95, 112
Sarangthem, Sanatombi 102
Saree(s) 4, 9–10, 13, 49, 86, 121
Scarves 10
Sekmai police station 48–50, 52, 54
Self-employment 80
Self-empowerment 42
Self-esteem xiv, 4, 15, 102, 147
Self-reliance xiv–xv, xvii, 13, 46, 55, 70
Self-respect 4, 70, 102, 147
Self-worth xiv, 102, 147
Sewing 38–39, 44, 55
Shawl(s) and Stole(s) xiii–xiv, 1–2, 7, 10–14, 16, 32, 40, 42, 69, 71–75, 79, 86–89, 99, 131, 140–41
  cotton 7, 32
  haophee 32, 40, 74
  inaphee 9, 40, 60, 111, 115, 133
  khwang 40, 73–74
  kukiphee 40
  ladies' 9, 13
  leiroom 2, 16, 40, 94
  lui 40, 73
  maflar 40
  shaphee lanphee 11
  stock of 72
  traditional xiv, 11–12, 32, 40, 74, 79, 87
  white 12–13, 73
  woollen xiii, 1–2, 16, 32, 40, 42, 69, 72, 75, 87, 89
Sidabi Ima Keithel 86
Silk 12–13, 42, 79, 86–87, 115
Singh, Jarnail xvii, 83–85
Singh, Oinam Gambhir 58
Singing 2, 95, 125, 133
Skill(s) xv, 10, 13, 15, 29, 32, 39–42, 55, 59, 61, 104, 120, 127
Sobita, Aunt 7
Song(s) 28, 52, 94, 97, 107–08, 130
Sonia Oinam (Bem)
  academic performance 46
  as a sub-divisional officer (SDO) at Patsoi 109
  career 6, 136
  childhood memories 8
  cleared the Manipur Civil Service examination 109
  doctoral degree (PhD) at Manipur University 102
  enrolled in No.1 Squadron, Senior Air Wing NCC Unit, Imphal 129
  fear of death 125
  Ima's encouragement 129
  life 97
  marriage 14, 19, 136–37
  my National Cadet Corps (NCC) classes and activities 96
  postgraduate studies in Life Sciences 130, 134
  sales and weaving network 33
  selected as an SSA primary teacher 135
  skills in weaving and embroidery 15
  struggles 14, 40, 130
  turning point in life 15

Spinning 4, 28, 34–36
Spinning wheels 4, 34, 36
Stitching 2, 16
Storytelling xvi, 29
Struggle(s) xiii–xvi, 2, 4, 7, 14, 20, 22, 26, 29, 41, 44, 48, 51, 71, 82, 90, 98–99, 104–06, 124, 130–31, 133, 136, 145–47
  common xv, 145
  emotional 41
  daily 146–47
  inner xiv, 41
  mental 145
  personal 7, 145
  physical 29
Sushila, Bamon 24, 34
Sweaters 28

Taj Mahal, Agra 124
Tangkhuls 74
Tareng (wooden spinning wheel) 4, 28, 36–37
Temples 54, 98, 101, 111–14
Tender marups 35
Textiles 12, 76
Thabal Chongba 56, 58
Thambalngou, Aunt 88
Thambalngou, Iche 88
Thangal Bazaar 86, 131
Thonipui laikot phaizols 13
Thoubal 72
Thumok (hand-woven traditional bamboo basket) 28
Tiken Oinam, Lieutenant xvi, 48, 66, 69, 120–21
  as Senior Under Officer (SUO) 120
Tirth mapan(s) 111, 113
Tolumu, Kshetrimayum 1
Tonshiza, Kshetrimayum Ongbi 1
Tourism Department, Government of Manipur 96
Towels 10, 87
Trade and exchange 33, 64, 75, 78, 82
  internal 82
Traders 33, 78, 82, 89, 103
  Bengalee 82
Tradition(s) 26–27, 29, 62, 64, 72–73, 76, 88, 92–93, 112, 118, 133–34, 137, 141, 146
  Meitei 26–27, 62, 92–93, 133, 137, 141
  weaving 72
Transaction(s) 38–39, 74–75, 78, 85, 89, 104
  monetary 75
Tribe(s) 12–13, 82
Trousseau(s) 10, 15, 32, 88, 94

Unemployment 56
Usharani, Oinam 56
Utensils 27, 45, 59, 81, 86–88, 94

Vaishnavism 5, 68, 95, 112
Vayu Sainik Camp 118, 129–30
Vegetables and fruits 1–2, 4, 25, 27, 43, 45, 53, 59, 62–63, 76, 78, 82, 86, 93, 109, 115–17, 122, 131, 140
Vendor(s) xiii, 32–34, 38–40, 42, 72–74, 77–80, 84–90, 146
  cards 86
  fellow 87–90
  registered 78, 86
  street 78, 79
  women 32, 34, 38, 42, 72–74, 78–80, 84–87, 146
  younger 87–88
Vision IAS Study Circle 131–32, 136

Waisheng Leima 76
Waithou Leima 76
Widows 70, 81, 146
Willpower xv, 42, 144
Work is worship xv, 105

Yailen, second baby 110, 141
Yaiphaba Longjam, husband xvii, 136
Yarn(s) 12, 28, 33–38, 74, 87

About the Author

SONIA OINAM, born in Imphal, Manipur, completed her BSc in Zoology (Hons) from Ghanapriya Women's College before pursuing a Master's degree in Life Sciences from Manipur University. Her doctoral research titled "Nematode Fauna of Cold-Blooded Vertebrates of Manipur" earned her a PhD from the same university. Since 2012, Sonia has been an integral part of the Manipur Civil Service and is currently serving as Joint Secretary to the Government of Manipur.

Sonia has always been passionate about writing, with a particular interest in articles, poetry, and memoirs. Her debut publication, *Endless I Will Be* (2023), is an anthology of poems that delve into emotions, exploration, and hope, capturing the essence of life.